TOM JACKSON'S

RESUME
EXPRESS

Also by Tom Jackson

The Hidden Job Market (with Davidyne Mayleas)
The Perfect Resume
Guerrilla Tactics in the Job Market
Not Just Another Job
Interview Express (with Bill Buckingham)
The Perfect Job Search
Perfect Resume Strategies (with Ellen Jackson)

TOM JACKSON'S
RESUME
EXPRESS

Tom Jackson and Bill Buckingham

TIMES BOOKS

RANDOM HOUSE

To all of our friends whose inspiration and support have enriched our lives, especially Ron Komrowski (1951–1993) and Michael Flannagan (1935–1993).

Library of Congress Cataloging-in-Publication Data

Jackson, Tom.
    Tom Jackson's resume express / by Tom Jackson, Bill Buckingham.—1st ed.
       p. cm.
     ISBN 0–8129–2128–3
     1. Resumes (Employment) 2. Applications for positions.
I. Buckingham, Bill. II. Title. III. Title: Resume express.
HF5383.J265 1993
650.14—dc20   92–56821

Manufactured in the United States of America

9   8   7   6   5   4   3   2

First Edition

Design and production by ROBERT BULL DESIGN

CONTENTS

MICHAEL WALSH
24 Grant Avenue
San Francisco, CA 94111
(415) 555-3847

JOB TARGET: Travel Consultant—Internal Corporate Accounts

CAPABILITIES:

- Access computer reservation/ticketing systems on the PARS, SABRE, and APOLLO networks.
- Respond to client requests and immediate needs for information on travel services.
- Plan itineraries for individuals and groups, coordinating travel, lodging, dining, and sight-seeing services.
- Administer client and vendor contacts, invoicing, sales reports, and accounts receivable.
- Fluent in French and Spanish with a working knowledge of Italian.

ACCOMPLISHMENTS:

- Consulted with hundreds of individual clients, corporations, and other organizations to coordinate travel needs.
- Designed travel itineraries for over 75 group tours with destinations in France, Russia, Brazil, Egypt, and Indonesia.
- Traveled extensively throughout the United States, Europe, the Mediterranean, Egypt, and the Orient; researched and explored areas with historical and cultural value.
- Managed office operations and staff for five-person agency, increasing staff efficiency while making significant reductions in overhead.

WORK HISTORY:

1990 – present	OAKLAND CIVIC CENTER Assistant Box Office Manager	Oakland, CA
1985 – 1989	ARC TRAVEL, Inc. Travel Consultant	Los Angeles, CA

EDUCATION:

1988	TWA TRAVEL COLLEGE	Kansas City, MO
1974	PACE UNIVERSITY AMDA program in Theater Education	New York, NY

DO IT NOW!

This book helps you jump right into the task of writing your resume without getting bogged down in philosophy and theory. Your goal is to write a great resume *now* and *Resume Express* is focused on that goal.

The Targeted Resume

THE HOTTEST RESUME IN TOWN!

There are a number of different approaches to putting together a resume. Each approach (or format) has its distinct advantages and disadvantages, but one resume format surpasses all the rest and has produced more interviews than any other we've seen. This is the *targeted* resume.

The targeted resume looks to the future. It's based on where you are going, not where you've been. It commands attention from employers by focusing on their needs and communicating the value and benefits you offer. And it is very easy to put together. You don't have to be an expert writer or a resume guru to assemble a high-impact resume.

Pretend you are an employer and read the resume on the previous page with a view toward understanding how this person can assist you.

The applicant, Michael Walsh, is very clear about the job he is after. His resume highlights what he *can do* in the performance of his job target. It also tells you what he *has done* in his field. This resume is a picture of a successful travel consultant and works well for Michael, even though he is currently working in an unrelated job.

GETTING STARTED

Part One of this book builds your targeted resume. If you follow each step, the words will come easily.

Part Two looks at two alternative approaches for writing your resume, the *chronological* approach and the *functional* approach. If you choose, you can easily assemble one of these resumes by rearranging the information you created in Part One.

Part Three offers important strategies and tips for using your resume, writing a power cover letter, and conducting your job search like a master.

Throughout the book we include sample resumes. Each has a story to tell and demonstrates how the person used the resume to his or her advantage. Use these samples as models for your resume.

Sharpen your pencil. In a matter of minutes you will have a job-winning resume ready for final production.

PART ONE

Build
Your
Resume

EXPRESSING YOUR VALUE

The key to career success is the creation of value in the eyes of the employer. The more the employer believes he or she will benefit from hiring you, the more opportunities for better jobs and salaries will open up for you.

Employers are in the business of hiring the right people. This means people who can do the work that needs to be done in a way that will produce the best bottom-line results for the organization.

THE UNIVERSAL HIRING RULE:
Any employer will hire any individual if the employer is convinced that the hire will produce more value than it costs.

When you target your resume to a particular employer or industry, you can focus it in a way that clearly demonstrates how your abilities relate to real and immediate needs. This targeting sets your resume ahead of others that are too sweeping and general.

The targeted resume is aimed at a specific type of opportunity and communicates that you can do this job. It describes your accomplishments in a way that shows your ability to produce results.

During the next few minutes you will create a targeted resume aimed at a specific career area or job target. The process is simple and fast.

ONE BOW—MANY ARROWS

Since the targeted resume focuses directly on the employer's needs, each of your job targets requires a different resume. This may sound like a lot of work; however, you will find that once you complete your first resume, it is easy to adjust it to meet the needs of a different employer.

You have one bow, made of your capabilities and demonstrated accomplishments, and each resume serves as a different arrow aimed at a specific target.

Complete the following warm-up.

You can gain valuable insights to help you write your resume by looking at the job from the employer's point of view.

Imagine yourself as an employer. You must hire someone right away as a _____ (enter your specific job target).

You want the best person in this job—someone who will help you make your business or department a success. It must be someone who will help you with many day-to-day problems and tasks. Five of the most important *challenges* are:

1. _____ ,
2. _____ ,
3. _____ ,
4. _____ ,
5. _____ .

To solve these day-to-day challenges, you need someone with the right knowledge, training, skills, and abilities. The best candidate would have these *capabilities*:

(a) _____ ,
(b) _____ ,
(c) _____ ,
(d _____ ,
(e) _____ .

Finally, it takes a person with the right character and personality to perform well on this job. These include the *qualities* of…:

(f) _____ ,
(g) _____ ,
(h) _____ ,
(i) _____ ,
(j) _____ .

Starting Line

As you build your targeted resume, always keep in mind an employer's needs and perspective.

THE SIX RESUME BLOCKS

1	MICHAEL WALSH 24 Grant Avenue San Francisco, CA 94111 (415) 555-3847	**Contact Information**
2	JOB TARGET: Travel Consultant—Internal Corporate Accounts	**Job Target**
3	CAPABILITIES: • Access computer reservation/ticketing systems on the PARS, SABRE, and APOLLO networks. • Respond to client requests and immediate needs for information on travel services. • Plan itineraries for individuals and groups, coordinating travel, lodging, dining, and sight-seeing services. • Administer client and vendor contacts, invoicing, sales reports, and accounts receivable. • Fluent in French and Spanish with a working knowledge of Italian.	**Capabilities**
4	ACCOMPLISHMENTS: • Consulted with hundreds of individual clients, corporations, and other organizations to coordinate travel needs. • Designed travel itineraries for over 75 group tours with destinations in France, Russia, Brazil, Egypt, and Indonesia. • Traveled extensively throughout the United States, Europe, the Mediterranean, Egypt, and the Orient; researched and explored areas with historical and cultural value. • Managed office operations and staff for five-person agency, increasing staff efficiency while making significant reductions in overhead.	**Accomplishments**

5	WORK HISTORY:
	1990 – present OAKLAND CIVIC CENTER Oakland, CA
	                  Assistant Box Office Manager
	1985 – 1989 ARC TRAVEL, INC. Los Angeles, CA
	                  Travel Consultant
		Work History

6	EDUCATION: 1988 TWA TRAVEL COLLEGE Kansas City, MO 1974 PACE UNIVERSITY New York, NY AMDA program in Theater Education	**Education**

The targeted resume has six basic blocks of information, and each block communicates a message that is important for the employer to know.

Follow the instructions as you work through each block. When completed, you will have all the material you need to put together your resume in a variety of ways.

YOUR CONTACT INFORMATION

1	**MICHAEL WALSH** 24 Grant Avenue San Francisco, CA 94111 (415) 555-3847	**Contact Information**
2	JOB TARGET: Travel Consultant—Internal Corporate Accounts	
3	CAPABILITIES: • Access computer reservation/ticketing systems on the PARS, SABRE, and APOLLO networks. • Respond to client requests and immediate needs for information on travel services. • Plan itineraries for individuals and groups, coordinating travel, lodging, dining, and sight-seeing services. • Administer client and vendor contacts, invoicing, sales reports, and accounts receivable. • Fluent in French and Spanish with a working knowledge of Italian.	
4	ACCOMPLISHMENTS: • Consulted with hundreds of individual clients, corporations, and other organizations to coordinate travel needs. • Designed travel itineraries for over 75 group tours with destinations in France, Russia, Brazil, Egypt, and Indonesia. • Traveled extensively throughout the United States, Europe, the Mediterranean, Egypt, and the Orient; researched and explored areas with historical and cultural value. • Managed office operations and staff for five-person agency, increasing staff efficiency while making significant reductions in overhead.	
5	WORK HISTORY: 1990 – present OAKLAND CIVIC CENTER Oakland, CA Assistant Box Office Manager 1985 – 1989 ARC TRAVEL, Inc. Los Angeles, CA Travel Consultant	
6	EDUCATION: 1988 TWA TRAVEL COLLEGE Kansas City, MO 1974 PACE UNIVERSITY New York, NY AMDA program in Theater Education	

Your contact information appears at the top of the resume. Use your business name (avoid nicknames). Spell out words like *Street*, *Avenue*, *North*, etc. Include your home telephone number and area code. If you cannot be reached at home during business hours, include a contact phone or work phone. Use discretion when including a work phone; your current employer may not approve.

MICHAEL WALSH
24 Grant Avenue
San Francisco, CA 94111
(415) 555-3847

*Enter your name exactly as you want it
to appear on your resume.*

Name: _____

Address: _____

City, State, ZIP: _____

Home Phone: (_____) _____

Contact Phone: (_____) _____ *(Optional)*

Fax Phone: (_____) _____ *(Optional)*

YOUR JOB TARGET

MICHAEL WALSH
24 Grant Avenue
San Francisco, CA 94111
(415) 555-3847

2 | JOB TARGET: Travel Consultant—Internal Corporate Accounts | **Job Target**

CAPABILITIES:

3
- Access computer reservation/ticketing systems on the PARS, SABRE, and APOLLO networks.
- Respond to client requests and immediate needs for information on travel services.
- Plan itineraries for individuals and groups, coordinating travel, lodging, dining, and sight-seeing services.
- Administer client and vendor contacts, invoicing, sales reports, and accounts receivable.
- Fluent in French and Spanish with a working knowledge of Italian.

ACCOMPLISHMENTS:

4
- Consulted with hundreds of individual clients, corporations, and other organizations to coordinate travel needs.
- Designed travel itineraries for over 75 group tours with destinations in France, Russia, Brazil, Egypt, and Indonesia.
- Traveled extensively throughout the United States, Europe, the Mediterranean, Egypt, and the Orient; researched and explored areas with historical and cultural value.
- Managed office operations and staff for five-person agency, increasing staff efficiency while making significant reductions in overhead.

Your job target is the specific field or job title you are actively pursuing. The targeted resume gets *very* specific. By being specific, you stand out to employers who have the needs you can fill. Once you are certain about your target, it becomes obvious what to include and what to leave out.

Given the diversity of today's job market, you should have two or three different job targets. Consider aiming a slightly different resume at each target.

SAMPLES

Job Target: Travel Agent—Internal Corporate Accounts

Job Target: Tour Guide

Job Target: Theater Manager

Although you will have more than one job target, select one you want to use now for writing your resume (refer to the target you identified on page 5).

Job Target: _____

☞ *If you have a clear job target, move on to block 3 (page 11).*

If you did not have a specific job target in mind, start screening information in the general field or talk to people who can give you information and direction on jobs you would enjoy and have the skills to do successfully. Review the following list of sample job targets to stimulate your imagination.

Here is a short random list of job titles to get you thinking. Check any title that interests you even slightly.

___ Account Executive	___ Customer Service Rep	___ Machinist	___ Reporter
___ Accountant	___ Dancer	___ Management Intern	___ Sales Representative
___ Administrative	___ Database	___ Market Analyst	___ Securities Broker
Assistant	Administrator	___ Marketing Coordinator	___ Social Director
___ Advertising Executive	___ Decorator/Artist	___ Mechanic	___ Social Worker
___ Agriculturist	___ Designer	___ Meteorologist	___ Software Designer
___ Appliance	___ Dietitian	___ Musician	___ Sound Engineer
Demonstrator	___ Elder-care Worker	___ Nurse	___ Speech Therapist
___ Auditor	___ Fabric Worker	___ Nutritionist	___ Systems Analyst
___ Bank Officer	___ Fashion Retailer	___ Occupational	___ Teacher
___ Bookkeeper	___ Field Worker	Therapist	___ Telemarketer
___ Budget Manager	___ Food Scientist	___ Office Manager	___ Translator
___ Buyer	___ Furniture Maker	___ Office Systems	___ Travel Agent
___ Circulation Manager	___ Grocery Employee	Designer	___ TV Production
___ Civil Engineer	___ Hospital Administrator	___ Paramedic	Assistant
___ Computer	___ Hotel Manager	___ Personnel Manager	___ Veterinarian
Programmer	___ Image Consultant	___ Physical Therapist	___ X-Ray Technician
___ Consumer Advocate	___ Instructor	___ Product Manager	___ Zoologist
___ Cook	___ Insurance Salesperson	___ Purchasing Agent	
___ Copy Editor	___ Interior Designer	___ Receptionist	

Add your own:

YOUR CAPABILITIES

MICHAEL WALSH
24 Grant Avenue
San Francisco, CA 94111
(415) 555-3847

JOB TARGET: Travel Consultant—Internal Corporate Accounts

3

CAPABILITIES:

- Access computer reservation/ticketing systems on the PARS, SABRE, and APOLLO networks.
- Respond to client requests and immediate needs for information on travel services.
- Plan itineraries for individuals and groups, coordinating travel, lodging, dining, and sight-seeing services.
- Administer client and vendor contacts, invoicing, sales reports, and accounts receivable.
- Fluent in French and Spanish with a working knowledge of Italian.

Capabilities

4

ACCOMPLISHMENTS:

- Consulted with hundreds of individual clients, corporations, and other organizations to coordinate travel needs.
- Designed travel itineraries for over 75 group tours with destinations in France, Russia, Brazil, Egypt, and Indonesia.
- Traveled extensively throughout the United States, Europe, the Mediterranean, Egypt, and the Orient; researched and explored areas with historical and cultural value.
- Managed office operations and staff for five-person agency, increasing staff efficiency while making significant reductions in overhead.

5

WORK HISTORY:

| 1990 – present | OAKLAND CIVIC CENTER Assistant Box Office Manager | Oakland, CA |
| 1985 – 1989 | ARC TRAVEL, Inc. Travel Consultant | Los Angeles, CA |

6

EDUCATION:

| 1988 | TWA TRAVEL COLLEGE | Kansas City, MO |
| 1974 | PACE UNIVERSITY AMDA program in Theater Education | New York, NY |

Your resume must communicate your ability to do the job. A capability is something you know you can do in the future. In this block of your resume you will list five to eight concise statements describing what you *can* do (whether or not you have done it so far) or *could* do in the performance of your selected job target.

Think about the key challenges or tasks the employer needs to have done (refer to your comments on page 5). What can you do for the employer that will help get the job done better, faster, more efficiently, at less cost?

*Notice how these capability statements
support the job target.*

JOB TARGET: Travel Consultant—Internal Corporate Accounts

CAPABILITIES:

- Access computer reservation/ticketing systems on the PARS, SABRE, and APOLLO networks.
- Respond to client requests and immediate needs for information on travel services.
- Plan itineraries for individuals and groups, coordinating travel, lodging, dining, and sight-seeing services.
- Administer client and vendor contacts, invoicing, sales reports, and accounts receivable.
- Fluent in French and Spanish with a working knowledge of Italian.

PASS 1: *Check any word that relates to something you* can *do in your job target area and want to highlight on your resume.*

I CAN...

____ Accelerate	____ Achieve	____ Acquire	____ Administer	____ Advise
____ Analyze	____ Arbitrate	____ Arrange	____ Assemble	____ Assist
____ Audit	____ Broaden	____ Budget	____ Build	____ Calculate
____ Chart	____ Collect	____ Complete	____ Compose	____ Conceive
____ Conduct	____ Conserve	____ Construct	____ Consult	____ Contribute
____ Control	____ Coordinate	____ Correspond	____ Counsel	____ Create
____ Critique	____ Delegate	____ Deliver	____ Demonstrate	____ Design
____ Detect	____ Determine	____ Develop	____ Devise	____ Diagnose
____ Direct	____ Discover	____ Dispense	____ Disprove	____ Distribute
____ Draw	____ Draw up	____ Edit	____ Eliminate	____ Establish

____ Evaluate	____ Examine	____ Execute	____ Expand	____ Expedite
____ Formulate	____ Generate	____ Guide	____ Hire	____ Identify
____ Implement	____ Improve	____ Increase	____ Initiate	____ Install
____ Institute	____ Instruct	____ Interpret	____ Interview	____ Introduce
____ Invent	____ Investigate	____ Launch	____ Lead	____ Lecture
____ Log	____ Maintain	____ Manage	____ Monitor	____ Motivate
____ Navigate	____ Negotiate	____ Network	____ Observe	____ Obtain
____ Operate	____ Order	____ Organize	____ Oversee	____ Perform
____ Plan	____ Prepare	____ Prescribe	____ Present	____ Prevent
____ Process	____ Produce	____ Program	____ Promote	____ Propose
____ Protect	____ Provide	____ Purchase	____ Receive	____ Recommend
____ Record	____ Recruit	____ Reduce	____ Refer	____ Render
____ Report	____ Represent	____ Research	____ Restore	____ Reverse
____ Review	____ Revise	____ Reward	____ Route	____ Save
____ Select	____ Sell	____ Serve	____ Set up	____ Sign
____ Solve	____ Strategize	____ Structure	____ Study	____ Supervise
____ Supply	____ Teach	____ Test	____ Train	____ Translate
____ Upgrade	____ Utilize	____ Win	____ Work with	____ Write

Add your own:

PASS 2: *You identified on page 5 five key capabilities that the employer would look for in a successful candidate (lines a through e). Review this list and think again about the most important skills, knowledge, or abilities you could contribute to the job. Write them on the lines below.*

_____

_____

_____

_____

_____

_____

PASS 3: *Review the words you checked in Pass 1 and the key capabilities you identified in Pass 2. Complete five to eight statements that clearly communicate your skills, knowledge, or ability to do the job.*

Regarding my job target as a _____:

(enter your job target)

I can: _____

_____

I can: _____

_____

I can: _____

_____

I can: _____

_____

I can: _____

_____

I can: _____

_____

I can: _____

_____

I can: _____

_____

Final Review

Review, edit, and rewrite your capability statements. Do they clearly communicate that you are able to add significant value in your job target field?

BE A 5-STAR CANDIDATE!

Today's employers are attracted to people who exhibit particular characteristics. Edit your capability statements to emphasize these qualities.

★ Confidence in times of uncertainty
★ Quick learning skills
★ Communication that spurs action in others
★ Creativity and innovativeness
★ Ability to motivate others
★ Concern for customers
★ Orientation toward quality work
★ A healthy competitive drive
★ Global thinking beyond old boundaries
★ Able to handle complexity
★ Willingness to promote diversity

YOUR ACCOMPLISHMENTS

MICHAEL WALSH
24 Grant Avenue
San Francisco, CA 94111
(415) 555-3847

JOB TARGET: Travel Consultant—Internal Corporate Accounts

CAPABILITIES:

- Access computer reservation/ticketing systems on the PARS, SABRE, and APOLLO networks.
- Respond to client requests and immediate needs for information on travel services.
- Plan itineraries for individuals and groups, coordinating travel, lodging, dining, and sight-seeing services.
- Administer client and vendor contacts, invoicing, sales reports, and accounts receivable.
- Fluent in French and Spanish with a working knowledge of Italian.

ACCOMPLISHMENTS:

- Consulted with hundreds of individual clients, corporations, and other organizations to coordinate travel needs.
- Designed travel itineraries for over 75 group tours with destinations in France, Russia, Brazil, Egypt, and Indonesia.
- Traveled extensively throughout the United States, Europe, the Mediterranean, Egypt, and the Orient; researched and explored areas with historical and cultural value.
- Managed office operations and staff for five-person agency, increasing staff efficiency while making significant reductions in overhead.

4 **Accomplishments**

WORK HISTORY:

5

1990 – present	OAKLAND CIVIC CENTER	Oakland, CA
	Assistant Box Office Manager	
1985 – 1989	ARC TRAVEL, Inc.	Los Angeles, CA
	Travel Consultant	

EDUCATION:

6

1988	TWA TRAVEL COLLEGE	Kansas City, MO
1974	PACE UNIVERSITY	New York, NY
	AMDA program in Theater Education	

An accomplishment is a result, contribution, or achievement you are responsible for in a particular job or activity. You have produced accomplishments in every area of your life: past or current jobs, school projects, volunteer work. Accomplishments create a positive picture and are hard to ignore.

This section of your resume demonstrates that you can produce results in your job target area that also underline your capabilities.

Notice how these accomplishment statements
support the job target.

JOB TARGET: Travel Consultant—Internal Corporate Accounts

ACCOMPLISHMENTS:

- Consulted with hundreds of individual clients, corporations, and other organizations to coordinate travel needs.
- Designed travel itineraries for over 75 group tours with destinations in France, Russia, Brazil, Egypt, and Indonesia.
- Traveled extensively throughout the United States, Europe, the Mediterranean, Egypt, and the Orient; researched and explored areas with historical and cultural value.
- Managed office operations and staff for 5-person agency, increasing staff efficiency while making significant reductions in overhead.

In describing your past work, make the distinction between accomplishments and duties. Duties are what your job *required* you to do. Accomplishments are the *tangible results* you produced. Every job has *duties*, but *accomplishments* are unique.

PASS 1: *To get your mind thinking about your accomplishments, check any word that reminds you of something you have done.*

____ Accelerated	____ Achieved	____ Acquired	____ Administered	____ Advised
____ Analyzed	____ Arbitrated	____ Arranged	____ Assembled	____ Assisted
____ Audited	____ Broadened	____ Budgeted	____ Built	____ Calculated
____ Charted	____ Collected	____ Completed	____ Composed	____ Conceived
____ Conducted	____ Conserved	____ Constructed	____ Consulted	____ Contributed
____ Controlled	____ Coordinated	____ Corresponded	____ Counseled	____ Created
____ Critiqued	____ Delegated	____ Delivered	____ Demonstrated	____ Designed
____ Detected	____ Determined	____ Developed	____ Devised	____ Diagnosed
____ Directed	____ Discovered	____ Dispensed	____ Disproved	____ Distributed
____ Drew	____ Drew up	____ Edited	____ Eliminated	____ Established
____ Evaluated	____ Examined	____ Executed	____ Expanded	____ Expedited
____ Formulated	____ Generated	____ Guided	____ Hired	____ Identified
____ Implemented	____ Improved	____ Increased	____ Initiated	____ Installed
____ Instituted	____ Instructed	____ Interpreted	____ Interviewed	____ Introduced
____ Invented	____ Investigated	____ Launched	____ Led	____ Lectured
____ Logged	____ Maintained	____ Managed	____ Monitored	____ Motivated
____ Navigated	____ Negotiated	____ Networked	____ Observed	____ Obtained
____ Operated	____ Ordered	____ Organized	____ Oversaw	____ Performed
____ Planned	____ Prepared	____ Prescribed	____ Presented	____ Prevented
____ Processed	____ Produced	____ Programmed	____ Promoted	____ Proposed
____ Protected	____ Provided	____ Purchased	____ Received	____ Recommended
____ Recorded	____ Recruited	____ Reduced	____ Referred	____ Rendered
____ Reported	____ Represented	____ Researched	____ Restored	____ Reversed
____ Reviewed	____ Revised	____ Rewarded	____ Routed	____ Saved
____ Selected	____ Sold	____ Served	____ Set up	____ Signed
____ Solved	____ Strategized	____ Structured	____ Studied	____ Supervised
____ Supplied	____ Taught	____ Tested	____ Trained	____ Translated
____ Upgraded	____ Utilized	____ Won	____ Worked with	____ Wrote

Add your own:

PASS 2: *In each category on the next few pages write down as many personal accomplishments and contributions as you can remember. Keep in mind the type of accomplishments that would capture the interest of an employer in your job target field. Use the words you checked in Pass 1 as a guide.*

Accomplishments from your **MOST RECENT WORK (PAID OR UNPAID) EXPERIENCE THAT SUPPORTS YOUR CAPABILITIES** (page 14).

Position (from _____ to _____) :

_____

In this work, I have: _____

_____

_____

_____

_____

Accomplishments from an **EARLIER WORK EXPERIENCE.**
Previous position (from _____ to _____) :

_____

In this work, I have: _____

_____

_____

_____

_____

Accomplishments from an **EARLIER WORK EXPERIENCE.**
Previous position (from _____ to _____) :

_____

In this work, I have: _____

_____

_____

_____

_____

Accomplishments from **PARTICIPATING IN PROFESSIONAL ASSOCIATIONS OR ORGANIZATIONS.**
In this area, I have:

_____

_____

_____

_____

Accomplishments from **SCHOOL OR OTHER TRAINING PROGRAMS.**
In this area, I have:

_____

_____

_____

_____

Accomplishments from **PARTICIPATING IN EXTRACURRIC-ULAR ACTIVITIES.**
In this area, I have:

_____

_____

_____

_____

Accomplishments from **COMMUNITY OR VOLUNTEER WORK.**
In this work, I have:

_____

_____

_____

_____

Accomplishments from **LEISURE-TIME ACTIVITIES OR HOB-BIES.**
I have:

_____

_____

_____

_____

Special **AWARDS, HONORS, OR RECOGNITION.**
I have been acknowledged for:

_____

_____

_____

_____

Before writing your accomplishment statements for your resume, consider these four guidelines:

- Keep each statement short.
- Start each statement with an action word such as those listed in Pass 1 (page 18).
- Quantify results you produced (how much? how many? how often?).
- Ask this, "Would an employer be interested in knowing that I did this?" If the answer is no, do not include it in your resume.

BE A 5-STAR CANDIDATE!

The best accomplishment statements demonstrate that you created value for others. Relate your accomplishments to your capabilities, although a direct connection is not necessary. Your accomplishments should create a picture of past successes that translate to future successes in the prospective employer's mind. Here are nine things most employers look for. Think of an accomplishment that shows you have:

★ Generated revenue (introduced new products, new markets, new sales)
★ Cut costs (reduced overhead, purchased intelligently, pared down unnecessary expenses)
★ Increased productivity (developed more efficient work systems, training programs, service plans)
★ Innovated (challenged traditional methods, improved packaging and design)
★ Improved quality (enhanced value to customers, reduced defects, increased service)
★ Saved time (improved work flow, eliminated steps)
★ Focused on customers (enhanced customer satisfaction)
★ Used technology (computerized an office system, used E mail, trained others in using technology)
★ Motivated others (got people to collaborate and cooperate)

PASS 3: *Looking at the capabilities you listed on page 14, and the accomplishments you listed in Pass 2, select five to eight accomplishments you produced that support your capabilities and will be of interest to employers in your job target area.*

Regarding my job target as a _____:

(enter your job target)

I have: _____

_____

I have: _____

_____

I have: _____

_____

I have: _____

_____

I have: _____

_____

I have: _____

_____

I have: _____

_____

I have: _____

_____

Final Review

Review, edit, and rewrite your accomplishment statements. Do they communicate your ability to produce results? Do they support the capabilities you listed in block 3 (page 14)?

YOUR WORK HISTORY

<table>
<tr><td>✔</td><td colspan="3" style="text-align:center">MICHAEL WALSH
24 Grant Avenue
San Francisco, CA 94111
(415) 555-3847</td></tr>
<tr><td>✔</td><td colspan="3">JOB TARGET: Travel Consultant—Internal Corporate Accounts</td></tr>
</table>

CAPABILITIES:

- Access computer reservation/ticketing systems on the PARS, SABRE, and APOLLO networks.
- Respond to client requests and immediate needs for information on travel services.
- Plan itineraries for individuals and groups, coordinating travel, lodging, dining, and sight-seeing services.
- Administer client and vendor contacts, invoicing, sales reports, and accounts receivable.
- Fluent in French and Spanish with a working knowledge of Italian.

ACCOMPLISHMENTS:

- Consulted with hundreds of individual clients, corporations, and other organizations to coordinate travel needs.
- Designed travel itineraries for over 75 group tours with destinations in France, Russia, Brazil, Egypt, and Indonesia.
- Traveled extensively throughout the United States, Europe, the Mediterranean, Egypt, and the Orient; researched and explored areas with historical and cultural value.
- Managed office operations and staff for five-person agency, increasing staff efficiency while making significant reductions in overhead.

5 — **WORK HISTORY:**

			Work History
1990 – present	OAKLAND CIVIC CENTER Assistant Box Office Manager	Oakland, CA	
1985 – 1989	ARC TRAVEL, Inc. Travel Consultant	Los Angeles, CA	

6 — **EDUCATION:**

1988	TWA TRAVEL COLLEGE	Kansas City, MO
1974	PACE UNIVERSITY AMDA program in Theater Education	New York, NY

Your work history can include current or past jobs, part-time work, self-employment, volunteer work, special assignments, self-initiated projects, internships, and so on.

Start with your most recent experience and work back in time.

SAMPLE

WORK HISTORY:

1990–present	OAKLAND CIVIC CENTER Assistant Box Office Manager	Oakland, CA
1985–1989	ARC TRAVEL, INC. Travel Consultant	Los Angeles, CA

Enter the facts about your work history.

1. *Your most recent experience:*

Year Start	Year Finish	Company/organization	City, State

Position title (if any)

2. *The experience before that:*

Year Start	Year Finish	Company/organization	City, State

Position title (if any)

3. *The experience before that:*

Year Start	Year Finish	Company/organization	City, State

Position title (if any)

4. *The experience before that:*

Year Start	Year Finish	Company/organization	City, State

Position title (if any)

YOUR EDUCATION AND TRAINING

MICHAEL WALSH
24 Grant Avenue
San Francisco, CA 94111
(415) 555-3847

JOB TARGET: Travel Consultant—Internal Corporate Accounts

CAPABILITIES:
- Access computer reservation/ticketing systems on the PARS, SABRE, and APOLLO networks.
- Respond to client requests and immediate needs for information on travel services.
- Plan itineraries for individuals and groups, coordinating travel, lodging, dining, and sight-seeing services.
- Administer client and vendor contacts, invoicing, sales reports, and accounts receivable.
- Fluent in French and Spanish with a working knowledge of Italian.

ACCOMPLISHMENTS:
- Consulted with hundreds of individual clients, corporations, and other organizations to coordinate travel needs.
- Designed travel itineraries for over 75 group tours with destinations in France, Russia, Brazil, Egypt, and Indonesia.
- Traveled extensively throughout the United States, Europe, the Mediterranean, Egypt, and the Orient; researched and explored areas with historical and cultural value.
- Managed office operations and staff for five-person agency, increasing staff efficiency while making significant reductions in overhead.

WORK HISTORY:

| 1990 – present | OAKLAND CIVIC CENTER
Assistant Box Office Manager | Oakland, CA |
| 1985 – 1989 | ARC TRAVEL, Inc.
Travel Consultant | Los Angeles, CA |

6

EDUCATION:

| 1988 | TWA TRAVEL COLLEGE | Kansas City, MO |
| 1974 | PACE UNIVERSITY
AMDA program in Theater Education | New York, NY |

Education

This block lists the schools and training programs you have attended. Detail your most recent education—school, degree or program, and date completed.

Include additional information—relevant course work, special activities or projects, grade point average, research studies—that supports the case you have been making.

SAMPLE

EDUCATION:
1988   TWA TRAVEL COLLEGE   Kansas City, MO
1974   PACE UNIVERSITY   New York, NY
        AMDA program in Theater Education

Enter the facts about your education.

1. Your most recent degree/program:

_____ _____ _____
Year   School or college   City, State
Finish

         _____
         Degree/Area of study

2. Previous education (if applicable):

_____ _____ _____
Year   School or college   City, State
Finish

         _____
         Degree/Area of study

3. Other relevant education:

_____ _____ _____
Year   School or college   City, State
Finish

         _____
         Degree/Area of study

Other Training Programs:

_____ _____
Year   Course or program

_____ _____
Year   Course or program

_____ _____
Year   Course or program

_____ _____
Year   Course or program

PUTTING IT ALL TOGETHER

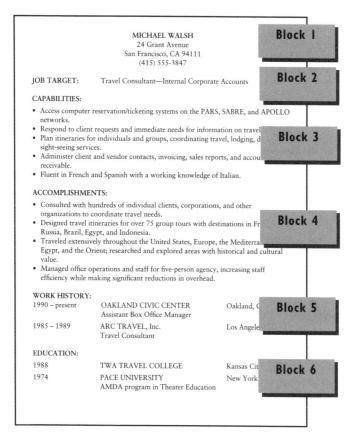

MICHAEL WALSH
24 Grant Avenue
San Francisco, CA 94111
(415) 555-3847

Block 1

JOB TARGET: Travel Consultant—Internal Corporate Accounts

Block 2

CAPABILITIES:

• Access computer reservation/ticketing systems on the PARS, SABRE, and APOLLO networks.
• Respond to client requests and immediate needs for information on travel
• Plan itineraries for individuals and groups, coordinating travel, lodging, d sight-seeing services.
• Administer client and vendor contacts, invoicing, sales reports, and accou receivable.
• Fluent in French and Spanish with a working knowledge of Italian.

Block 3

ACCOMPLISHMENTS:

• Consulted with hundreds of individual clients, corporations, and other organizations to coordinate travel needs.
• Designed travel itineraries for over 75 group tours with destinations in Fr Russia, Brazil, Egypt, and Indonesia.
• Traveled extensively throughout the United States, Europe, the Mediterra Egypt, and the Orient; researched and explored areas with historical and cultural value.
• Managed office operations and staff for five-person agency, increasing staff efficiency while making significant reductions in overhead.

Block 4

WORK HISTORY:

| 1990 – present | OAKLAND CIVIC CENTER
Assistant Box Office Manager | Oakland, C |
| 1985 – 1989 | ARC TRAVEL, Inc.
Travel Consultant | Los Angele |

Block 5

EDUCATION:

| 1988 | TWA TRAVEL COLLEGE | Kansas Cit |
| 1974 | PACE UNIVERSITY
AMDA program in Theater Education | New York |

Block 6

These next four steps show you how to assemble your targeted resume.

Step 1. Assemble Your Resume Draft

Now that you have all the information, it's time to assemble the resume blocks into an attractive, professional presentation.

The way your resume looks on the page—organization, layout, and printing—says something about you just as the way you dress for an interview does. Your resume represents you. A sloppy resume with spelling or grammar mistakes sends the message that you don't care about the quality of your work. A clear and organized resume tells the prospective employer that you put thought and attention into getting the job done right.

Your resume is a business communication. Keep it concise. If possible, limit your resume to one page. Remember: You can go into more detail during the interview. Lay it out on the page so it is easy to read.

Take out a few pieces of lined paper. Follow the instructions that begin below to block out your resume in rough-draft form.

GUIDELINES FOR ASSEMBLING YOUR RESUME:

Block 1: Center your name at the top of the sheet.

Block 2: Indicate your job target for this resume. (Prepare a different resume for each target.)

Block 3: List five to eight capability statements that illustrate that you *can* do what needs to be done in your job target area. Start each statement with a present-tense verb as if the statement were completing the sentence "I can..." Arrange your statements with the most important ones first.

Block 4: List five to eight accomplishment statements that demonstrate you *have* produced results in areas that would be of interest to a prospective employer and that support your capabilities. Start each statement with a past-tense verb as if the statement were completing the sentence "I have..." Arrange your statements with the most important ones first.

Block 5: List your work and nonwork experience in chronological order starting with your most recent experience. (You may omit this section entirely if you have no experience or your work history is spotty.)

Block 6: List your education starting with your most recent degree or qualification. *If you are just graduating or a particular degree is extremely important for the job, put this block right after your job target.*

Step 2. Critique Your Draft

First do a rough draft of your resume, then ask others to point out areas for improvement. Use the following checklist as a guide.

__ Does the material fit neatly on one page?

__ Are there any spelling, grammar, or punctuation errors?

__ Are all statements easily understood?

__ Are paragraphs and sentences short and to the point?

__ Have you repeated any information that you could consolidate?

__ Does the resume paint the best possible picture of you?

__ Would an employer immediately see the potential benefits you offer?

__ Does each capability and accomplishment statement start with a strong action word?

__ Have you eliminated extraneous information (height, weight, gender, health, marital status, salary history)?

__ Is the layout simple, professional, attractive, and easy to read?

Step 3. Producing Your Final Resume

Personal computers eliminate much of the labor in creating your resume. Word-processing programs and intelligent resume-writing software allow you to easily produce multiple versions of your resume for particular employers and for future updates.

• Use a top-quality word processor and laser printer with a clear, clean typeface. If you don't have a computer or word processor at home or in the office, you can lease or borrow one through libraries, counseling centers, community colleges, or copy shops. If you don't type, get someone to prepare the final proof.

• Keep it simple. Leave plenty of white space to make your resume easy to read. Use wide margins and double spacing between sections.

• Do not show off all the features on your laser printer. Keep everything in the same font (typeface). Highlight key information in boldface or by underlining (but don't go overboard). You can use a larger point size to set off your name or the headings, but that's all. Do not use graphics.

• Have someone other than the person who typed your final resume proofread it for spelling, grammar, and punctuation errors.

Step 4. Print Your Resume

- Make your final resumes top quality. Do not settle for anything less. Take your final version to a good local printer or high-quality copy shop, or use a laser printer.
- Use high-quality paper stock. Choose white, ivory, buff, or off-white. Do not use colored paper.
- If you are making multiple copies on a photocopying machine, inspect the first copy to make sure there are no specks or smudges.
- *Do not* produce your final resume on a home-quality portable typewriter, dot matrix printer, or inexpensive copy machine.

A Final Word!

Congratulations on your perseverance in creating a resume that communicates clarity, assertiveness, and value.

Always look for ways to upgrade the message you want to communicate on your resume. If this means rewriting your resume for a specific job opportunity, then do so. The more clearly you convey the value you offer, the more likely it is that you will be called in for an interview.

TEN JOB-WINNING TARGETED RESUMES

1. Juan Rincon
Software Programmer

2. Christopher Andrews
Manager—Advertising Department

3. David Gillam
Sales Representative

4. Gwen N. Berry
Community Relations Director

5. Lynne Ciani
Director of International Sales

6. Franklin Kempner
Body-Building Consultant

7. Ronda Jackson
Order Processing Clerk

8. Shirley Warner
Director of Development

9. Thomas Bork
Video Production

10. William Cooper
Business Administration

JUAN RINCON

SOFTWARE PROGRAMMER

Juan was employed in a small manufacturing firm, performing clerical and shipping and receiving duties.

He was also an electronics student with a passionate hobby and some real talent with computer programming.

Out of his hobby, Juan had developed skills that could be sold to a new employer; however, he had no real paid work experience as a software programmer.

Because of his interest, Juan knew a great deal about what's expected of a programmer. He knew what *capabilities* to write without even having to do extensive research.

Notice Juan had nothing from his current paid position listed. He wrote only about his skills and understanding of his job target, which was in fact his *hobby*.

JUAN RINCON
766 Porter Avenue
Columbus, OH 43219
(614) 555-2334

JOB TARGET: Software Programmer

CAPABILITIES:

- Program IBM PC and compatibles in DOS and Windows environments.
- Design user interface in software programs that incorporate easy-to-follow logical progression of steps.
- Program software in C, C++, Visual BASIC, and Pascal.
- Design and produce computer-generated graphics.
- Operate DOS machines and peripherals; diagnose and fix hardware problems.
- Operate a variety of software programs including most major authoring systems, word processors, database programs, spreadsheet and graphics packages.

ACCOMPLISHMENTS:

- Designed and programmed an attendance/registration database program for the Ohio School of Electronics.
- Created six utility programs that have been distributed through the Shareware network; received over two thousand registrations from satisfied users.
- Won Golden Disk Award (utilities category) for 1991.
- Established the Central Ohio PC User's Group; increased membership from 10 to 235 individuals in four years.
- Created and maintained an on-line 24-hour bulletin board for the PC user's group.

WORK HISTORY:

| 1989 – present | WAYLAND PLASTICS, INC.
Assistant Manager —Shipping | Columbus, OH |
| 1986 – 1989 | OHIO SCHOOL OF ELECTRONICS
Registration Clerk (work-study) | Columbus, OH |

EDUCATION:

| 1989 | OHIO SCHOOL OF ELECTRONICS | Columbus, OH |

CHRISTOPHER ANDREWS
MANAGER—ADVERTISING DEPARTMENT

Christopher had a good work history in the same field. He could have written a chronological resume with no gaps, demonstrating career growth.

However, he was dead-ended in his current company, and he was looking not only to move out but also to move up.

He chose the targeted format so that he could demonstrate an understanding of his field in a broader way than just within the television industry.

In the *capabilities* section, he also was able to include other skills, like fluency in speaking and writing Spanish.

He also had several short stints of part-time self-employment, but because they added nothing new to his credentials, he left them out of his work history.

CHRISTOPHER ANDREWS
46076 Bell Road
Scottsdale, AZ 85251
(602) 555-3412

JOB TARGET: Manager of Advertising Department

CAPABILITIES:

- Consult with clients, initiate sales and services, and negotiate contracts.
- Initiate, design, and orchestrate all creative points in the development of advertising campaigns utilizing a diversity of media: video, animation of all print, and computer-generated art and graphics.
- Organize and manage all aspects and details in the execution of the projects from start through completion.
- Manage and supervise advertising and design units.
- Speak and write Spanish fluently.

ACCOMPLISHMENTS:

- Organized, planned, and executed the design, schedule, and direction for over 42 catalogs, direct-mail pieces, brochures, and other print materials.
- Planned and art-directed commercial photography and video sessions for major commercial clients, television and video producers, retail catalogers and retail industry, utilizing multiformats.
- Art-directed and coordinated a multimedia campaign for an international television film series with the United States and Spain; designed the promotional package and secured $2 million in funding for this project.
- Automated the design department for Arizona Public Television with new hardware/software purchases that generated a 150% increase in production rates for an extensive client base.
- Conducted negotiations with printers and other vendors that resulted in a 15% cost savings over previous years.

WORK HISTORY:

1991 – present	Arizona Public Television	Phoenix, AZ
	Associate Manager of Advertising Services	
1986 – 1991	Desert Graphics, Inc.	Phoenix, AZ
	Advertising Production Assistant	

EDUCATION:

1986	EASTERN MICHIGAN UNIVERSITY	Ypsilanti, MI
	B.A. in Business Administration and Marketing	
1980	ST. CLAIR COMMUNITY COLLEGE	Port Huron, MI
	Commercial Art and Computer Graphics	

DAVID GILLAM

SALES REPRESENTATIVE

David was a graduating senior whose job target was not connected to his degree. He had several years of solid summer work experience.

He wanted to turn his sales skills from summer work into his full-time job target. His *capabilities* section allowed him to state his wide understanding of a generic sales representative position.

His *accomplishments* section reflected real data, even if only from short spurts of work.

He also had the latitude to add additional college-learned skills, like his PC training and experience in his *capabilities* section.

It was perfectly okay to list all the jobs as summer work experience. Given such a short work history, David still had enough achievements for which to be proud.

DAVID GILLAM
6 Front Street #6C
Cedar Rapids, IA 52402
(319) 555-3990

JOB TARGET: Sales Representative

EDUCATION:

1993   IOWA STATE UNIVERSITY   Cedar Rapids, IA
               B.A. in Communication Arts

CAPABILITIES:

- Sell and promote a variety of products to individuals or companies on a cold-call basis.
- Establish customer base in a familiar or unfamiliar territory within a short period of time.
- Instruct and train new employees.
- Exhibit leadership and motivational abilities.
- Communicate effectively with people in a sales and customer-relations atmosphere.
- Work on IBM PC or Macintosh computers; operate word-processing, database, and spreadsheet programs.

ACCOMPLISHMENTS:

- Sold educational books on a door-to-door basis; placed orders, handled cash, and delivered. Grossed $7,600 in sales in a two-month period.
- Ranked 18th nationally out of more than 2,000 first-year dealers.
- Won Gold Seal Award for dealer who averaged 80-hour work week.
- Sold/rented water-treatment systems to homeowners and commercial businesses.
- Contacted business leaders throughout Iowa as part of marketing services of the International Business Club to promote cooperation and fellowship between Iowa and foreign businesses.

WORK HISTORY:

1989 – present Summers	CLEARWATER SYSTEMS, INC. Salesperson/Service Representative	Cedar Rapids, IA
1992	C.J.'s RESTAURANT Waiter	Cedar Rapids, IA
1990-1991 Summers	SOUTHERN PUBLISHING CO. Salesperson	Atlanta, GA

GWEN N. BERRY

COMMUNITY RELATIONS DIRECTOR

Gwen became a homemaker almost immediately upon graduating from college. She never developed a paid career outside the home.

However, for seven of the last fourteen years, Gwen amassed extensive volunteer experience and accomplishments that gave her a key to targeting her future job.

As a volunteer, Gwen absorbed plenty of background research to tell her how to focus herself and eventually pitch for a paid position.

Also, as with many volunteers, she developed an impressive list of accomplishments, which in terms of hard facts are as sales-worthy as anyone's who might have been paid to perform the same functions.

She changed the title *Work History* to *Experience* so as to include her volunteer affiliations.

GWEN N. BERRY
15 Northgate Street
Atlanta, GA 30341
(404) 555-8299

JOB TARGET: Community Relations Director

CAPABILITIES:
- Promote public understanding and support for programs and services.
- Organize and direct fund-raising campaigns.
- Write press releases, informational brochures, and other public relations materials.
- Give presentations, speeches, and workshops to public, private, and nonprofit organizations.
- Establish contacts with local print, radio, and TV news editors.
- Recruit and train volunteer workers.
- Prepare budgets, administer projects, and review results.

ACCOMPLISHMENTS:
- Built a personal contact network including CEOs and executive directors of over 50 local private businesses and community-service organizations.
- Coordinated the United Way Volunteer's Fund-raising Campaign that raised over $250,000 for health, education, and AIDS awareness programs.
- Recruited 2,000+ volunteers over the last six years to work in a variety of school-related programs.
- Won Distinguished Community Service Award from the Atlanta Cultural Affairs Commission.

EXPERIENCE:

1990 – present	UNITED WAY OF ATLANTA Community Services Volunteer	Atlanta, GA
1986 – 1992	ATLANTA METRO. SCHOOLS Member and chairperson of a variety of special volunteer programs	Atlanta, GA

EDUCATION:

1979	EMORY UNIVERSITY B.A. in English	Atlanta, GA

LYNNE CIANI

DIRECTOR OF INTERNATIONAL SALES

Lynne's company had been bought out twice before and she survived sales force layoffs in both staff reductions.

With the third buyout, a whole new sales force was coming on board. Lynne wanted not only to keep her job but also to move up from within.

The targeted resume gave her the power to show off how much she understood about the company itself and the demands of her new upgraded job target.

Lynne studied both the goals and the culture of the new owners and confidently put together a targeted resume.

She combined her achievements in the old company with her knowledge of what the future of the new company could bring, with herself in an expanded, higher position.

LYNNE CIANI
244 Kennedy Avenue
Boston, MA 02148
(617) 555-3456

JOB TARGET: Director of International Sales

CAPABILITIES:

- Utilize extensive knowledge of the Specialty Cheese/Supermarket Deli industry in the United States and Europe.
- Establish major accounts and manage regional brokers.
- Analyze sales statistics to develop specific objectives for accounts.
- Plan and formulate pricing programs to increase gross profitability.
- Develop and implement marketing strategies and design promotional programs.
- Train broker sales representatives and conduct seminars for supermarket account personnel.
- Fluent in French and Spanish.

ACCOMPLISHMENTS:

- Established and maintained accounts with over 35 major customers encompassing all major supermarket chains in New England and Upstate New York.
- Increased annual sales from $1.1 million to $5.5 million in four years.
- Planned and coordinated approximately $750,000 in co-op advertising funds annually.
- Planned and conducted "Cheese School" seminars at key accounts.
- Managed Cheese Department in a specialty gourmet shop for five years; developed extensive knowledge in product handling, merchandising, and customer relations.

WORK HISTORY:

1989 – present	GORDON–ROSS FOODS, INC. New England Sales Manager	Boston, MA
1985 – 1989	ROSS FOODS, INC. Telemarketer	Boston, MA
1980 – 1985	THE WINERY Assistant Store Manager	Santa Fe, NM

EDUCATION:

1979	SALEM STATE COLLEGE Marketing Management	Salem, MA

FRANKLIN KEMPNER

BODY-BUILDING CONSULTANT

Franklin was a successful chiropractor working in a family business. For years he had been doing body building as a hobby.

Franklin's long-term goal was to be a personal fitness trainer to individual clients and incorporate his chiropractic skills without having to run a full-time practice.

His interim job target was to affiliate with a gym where he could work part time on body building with individual members while continuing his chiropractic business.

He started with two clients as a personal fitness trainer, but listed it under his *work history*, giving it almost equal status with his chiropractic practice.

His *capabilities* section focuses almost exclusively on the needs of a health club, emphasizing the overall benefit of increasing membership—a club's prime need to stay in business.

FRANKLIN KEMPNER
116 Genesee Street
Rochester, NY 14610
(716) 555-9990

JOB TARGET: Body-Building Consultant

CAPABILITIES:

- Diagnose new and existing member health and fitness problems; prescribe comprehensive programs for meeting client needs.
- Set long-term goals for clients, promoting extended memberships.
- Increase club business, ensuring members' commitment and multiple referrals.
- Design beginner, intermediate, and advanced personal fitness programs with the added knowledge of medical disciplines.
- Instruct in the proper use of exercise equipment while demonstrating correct form and technique.
- Develop individualized manual therapeutic exercise programs.

ACCOMPLISHMENTS:

- As personal fitness trainer, consulted over 150 clients for more than three years.
- Diagnosed and treated sports-related injuries.
- Established and presented Sports Injury Awareness workshops in five high school athletic programs.
- Won the Junior Mr. Atlantic U.S.A. Body-Building Championship in 1985.
- Lectured for the Upstate Sports Massage Team, Rochester School of Ballet, and Onondaga County Community College.

WORK HISTORY:

1990 – Present	Personal Training Consultant	Rochester, NY
1987 – Present	Chiropractor—Private Practice	Rochester, NY
1985 – 1987	Syracuse City School System Health Education Instructor	Syracuse, NY

EDUCATION:

1987	Los Angeles Chiropractic College Doctorate
1985	Syracuse University B.S. in Health Education

RONDA JACKSON

ORDER PROCESSING CLERK

Ronda was midway through college, looking for a summer job.

It looked like there would be twelve clerical openings in a big factory in her town. The newspapers were suggesting there would probably be more than two hundred applicants.

Having studied the want ads for job descriptions, she decided to put herself ahead of the pack by focusing her campaign and her resume on the available openings in this specific factory.

Her *capabilities* section reflected both her past summer experience as well as her research on the new desired position. Her *accomplishments* section reflected a highly competent summer employee.

Rather than simply listing her past jobs chronologically, this resume format helped Ronda look more competitive. She had taken the time to do the research and could indicate how she could stretch into the job.

RONDA JACKSON
14458 North First Street
Rosemont, PA 19010
(215) 555-4928

JOB TARGET: Order Processing Clerk

CAPABILITIES:
- Handle customer contacts (walk-in, telephone, or correspondence); answer inquiries, resolve problems.
- Process mail or telephone orders.
- Key alpha and numeric data accurately and proficiently.
- Check completed invoices for accuracy; make corrections if necessary.
- Process orders and package merchandise.
- Determine the fastest and most cost-effective shipping method.
- Supervise order processing personnel; plan and assign work duties and monitor performance.

ACCOMPLISHMENTS:
- Sorted over 800 pieces of mail and other deliveries on a daily basis for a hospital mail room; delivered mail to offices and departments.
- Collected outgoing mail; processed UPS and overnight deliveries.
- Improved efficiency of mail room by decreasing the time to package, weigh, and address outgoing packages.
- Monitored staff of three part-time student workers.
- Served over 2,000 customers in a fast-food restaurant, fulfilling orders and taking payment.

WORK HISTORY:

1992 – 1993	BRYN MAWR HOSPITAL	Bryn Mawr, PA
	Mail Room Clerk	
1990 – 1991	BURGERS FOREVER	Ardmore, PA
	Counter Attendant	

EDUCATION:

| 1990 – present | BRYN MAWR COLLEGE | Bryn Mawr, PA |
| | Bachelor's Program in Sociology | |

SHIRLEY WARNER

DIRECTOR OF DEVELOPMENT

Shirley had a long, successful, professional career in development with one organization. Having garnered many loyal clients, Shirley wanted to break out on her own.

So after sixteen years, she took her contacts with her and opened up a small consulting business in her home.

But Shirley missed the camaraderie of working with others and the advantages of having a larger organization take care of the administrative headaches of running a business.

Having been away from an organization for a while, she actually had expanded her knowledge base of what was happening or about to happen in her field. She had a good sense of what to say in the *capabilities* section.

Her *accomplishments* included an undifferentiated list from the two positions.

SHIRLEY WARNER
655 North Lake Avenue
Detroit, MI 48221
(313) 555-4888

JOB TARGET: Director of Development

CAPABILITIES:

- Direct capital campaigns, feasibility studies, annual giving drives, and planned-giving programs.
- Write speeches, case statement brochures, and grant proposals.
- Conduct interviews, tabulate and analyze findings, write reports, and present conclusions and recommendations.
- Teach, advise, and counsel students on academic and personal concerns.

ACCOMPLISHMENTS:

- Organized and conducted a capital campaign to raise $600,000 in individual contributions for a private school in Detroit, MI; completed the campaign in less than four months and exceeded goals by 25%.
- Set up and implemented a planned-giving program in conjunction with a $4 million capital campaign for a not-for-profit hospital.
- Planned long-range development program to raise $300,000 (20% of operating expenses) for nonprofit arts organization. Wrote grants to secure additional $125,000 from county, state, and federal sources.
- Advised clients on integrating annual campaigns with capital campaigns as well as programs for securing special grants, major gifts, and planned or deferred gifts.

WORK HISTORY:

1991 – present	WARNER & ASSOCIATES Consulting Associate	Detroit, MI
1975 – 1991	WENTWORTH ACADEMY Director of Development (1982 – 1991) Assistant Development Director (1975 – 1982)	Detroit, MI

EDUCATION:

1974	PRINCETON UNIVERSITY M.B.A.	Princeton, NJ
1968	WAYNE STATE UNIVERSITY B.A. in French	Detroit, MI

THOMAS BORK

VIDEO PRODUCTION

Thomas wrote this resume as a graduating senior in college.

Aside from school projects, his part-time work experience was an unpaid barter arrangement managing a small off-campus apartment complex catering to local students.

Thomas's relevant experience came from managing various projects that were academic requirements for his degree. However, these school projects reflected a significant degree of accomplishment.

Since video production was a focused discipline within his degree, Thomas knew what was required within that job target. He therefore knew how to fill out the *capabilities* section.

As a new graduate with a relevant degree, *education* as a category is placed at the top after the *job target.*

THOMAS BORK
532 Mifflin Street
Madison, WI 53703
(608) 555-8902

JOB TARGET: Video Production

EDUCATION:

1993   UNIVERSITY OF WISCONSIN   Madison, WI
                    B.A. in Communication Arts

CAPABILITIES:

- Direct productions; tape and edit using super-8 film and 1/4" videotape.
- Operate TV cameras, video control console, and audio equipment.
- Monitor on-air programs to ensure technical quality of broadcasts.
- Operate sound-mixing board to control output of voices, sound effects, and music.

ACCOMPLISHMENTS:

- Assisted in preparation and striking of camera equipment on set of MTV music video; transported film between camera operators and film loaders.
- Performed grip functions on video commercial for Miller Brewing Company; operated various fog and light equipment and routed electrical hookups.
- Hosted weekly three-hour program for campus radio station.
- Produced audio commercials and print advertisements for radio station; created materials using various mixers, signal processors, and taping equipment.
- Wrote and recorded motivational song for national footwear company.

WORK HISTORY:

1990 – 1992	WLHA-FM Program Host/Disc Jockey	Madison, WI
1991	JOHN ROACH PROJECTS Grip	Madison, WI
1989 – 1991	TAMARACK APARTMENTS Resident Manager	Madison, WI

WILLIAM COOPER

BUSINESS ADMINISTRATION

William worked with a career counselor familiar with military conversions. He had loads of military experience that would translate to the private sector.

The biggest challenge for William was to learn the lingo of business and then see how his past accomplishments could have direct relevance in a business environment.

To research his *capabilities* section, William read a year's worth of business publications, including *The Wall Street Journal*.

He also conducted information interviews with friends and neighbors to collect ideas on their specific views of business trends and how and where he might fit in.

After absorbing all that information on the needs of business, William found that this format suited him best. His career counselor helped him reword the military accomplishments into business talk.

WILLIAM COOPER
6 Dalton Place
Dallas, TX 75265
(214) 555-3478

JOB TARGET: Business Administration

CAPABILITIES:

- Utilize expertise in organizational development and management, including strategic planning, decision making, problem solving, and creating organizational structure.
- Generate enthusiasm and unity of purpose to achieve goals.
- Manage total operations and logistics, including fiscal, administrative, and labor force.
- Coordinate instructional programs, including program planning, instructor training, and delivery.

ACCOMPLISHMENTS:

- Directed largest recruiting station in the Air Force with a staff of 132 and $1.3 million operational budget. Oversaw 42 subfacilities in a three-state area. Managed contracting, vendor services, and facilities.
- Procured 7.5% of total Air Force recruitment, regularly surpassing recruitment goals. Developed successful marketing plan, achieving 37% market share.
- Developed Air Force Recruitment Training Program from ground up, including program design, instructor training, and quality control. Increased enrollment from 3,000 to 15,000 in one year.
- Implemented systems, staff assignments, and management practices of educational training facilities to withstand 60% annual turnover in personnel.

WORK HISTORY:

1988 – 1993	U.S. AIR FORCE RECRUITING STATION Executive Officer	Tulsa, OK
1981 – 1988	U.S. AIR FORCE SCHOOLS Director of Educational Services	Dallas, TX

EDUCATION:

1986	INSTRUCTIONAL MANAGEMENT SCHOOL U.S. Air Force—Colorado Springs, CO
1984	COMMAND AND STAFF COLLEGE U.S. Air Force—Colorado Springs, CO
1980	WAKE FOREST UNIVERSITY, B.A.

PART TWO

Alternative
Approaches

ALTERNATIVE RESUME FORMATS

In Part One you put together a resume targeted to a very particular employer need—a job target. This targeted resume style emphasized your capabilities—the ability to create future value, supported by past accomplishments.

This approach is one we recommend because it focuses on future opportunity.

There are other, more conventional, ways to organize your resume information that you should consider. We present two of these formats here.

Review the *chronological* and *functional* resume discussions on the following pages. If you want to use one of these formats, it is relatively simple to rearrange the information you created in Part One.

The Chronological Resume

The *chronological* resume emphasizes your career path and experience. It describes the jobs you have held starting with the most recent. Each position includes a brief description of your contributions and accomplishments on the job.

This is the most traditional way to structure a resume and is familiar to most employers. It is a good approach if you have a job history that shows growth and development, and what you have done leads naturally to what you want to do next. It is not the best approach to take if you are just starting your career, your work history is spotty, or your experience is in a different area from your current job target.

Diane Owen chose the chronological format to highlight her sixteen years with one employer. Her resume shows an impressive career development within the organization as she was promoted from a divisional manager to a national sales manager.

DIANE OWEN
66 Washington Avenue
Reston, VA 44011
(703) 555-8893

JOB TARGET: Sales Management

WORK EXPERIENCE:

1978 – present   BLUERIDGE PRODUCTS, INC.   Alexandria, VA

1987 – present   National Sales Manager

- Managed $45 million of sales for food service and bakery company exceeding sales targets in both pounds and units.
- Increased profits 45% in last fiscal year.
- Managed 13 sales managers and 45 brokers nationally.
- Completely overhauled customer service department resulting in stronger communications between inside and outside teams.
- Conceived and implemented methods for substantially reducing unabsorbed freight and bringing $11,000 per month to the bottom line.

1984 – 1987   Sales Manager—Food Service Division

- Responsible for 75% of annual corporate sales.
- Launched new line as major marketing need for deli department in supermarket trade; added new products to fit in line.
- Instituted use of outside manufacturing sources to improve profitability of marginal products.

1978 – 1984   Eastern Divisional Manager

- Headed 5 east coast food service and bakery territories providing $25 million in annual sales; increased sales volume by 35%.
- Trained field regional managers and brokers.
- Dropped unprofitable direct retail sales division and incorporated into master distributor program.

EDUCATION:

1986   GEORGE MASON UNIVERSITY, Fairfax, VA
         M.B.A.

1978   GEORGE MASON UNIVERSITY, Fairfax, VA
         B.A. in English and History

The Functional Resume

The *functional* resume highlights your skills or areas of expertise. It gives little or no regard to when or where you attained the experience.

This is a particularly good approach if your job target requires specific, definable skills. It is not the best approach if you have a limited number of skills or if you want to emphasize growth in your career history.

Elizabeth Smith chose the functional format to highlight her skills. As a homemaker returning to the work force, she did not have a progressive career history. Her resume clearly demonstrates that her skills support her job target.

ELIZABETH SMITH
5895 Rhodes Avenue
St. Louis, Missouri 63109
(314) 555-4488

JOB TARGET: Job Training Counselor

COUNSELING:

- Coordinated corporate outplacement center.
- Assisted clients in conducting career evaluation while performing directive counseling.
- Developed clients' resumes and successful marketing strategies.
- Identified and researched potential employers and specific corporate hiring authorities.
- Provided psychological support for recently terminated employees.

ADMINISTRATIVE MANAGEMENT:

- Supervised office activities while ensuring efficient operation of small publishing and sales promotion company.
- Coordinated sales and management seminars throughout the U.S., including travel and facilities arrangements.
- Developed and maintained customer relations.
- Coordinated production and sales of books and other promotional and educational materials.

PUBLIC RELATIONS/COMMUNITY SERVICE:

- Assisted coordinator of special services for a national health organization.
- Promoted events and conducted public relations and fund-raising for a nationally recognized regional theater company.
- Coordinated volunteer activities, including recruitment, for a private hospital's major fund-raiser. Raised in excess of $150,000 annually.

WORK HISTORY:

1980 – present	Volunteer with MO Job Center, St. Louis, MO
	Volunteer with Children's Hospital, St. Louis, MO
	Fund-raiser, Loretto-Hilton Theater, Webster Groves, MO
Previous	UNIVERSITY OF ILLINOIS, Urbana, IL
	Assistant Copywriter, *Leviathan* Newsletter

EDUCATION:

| 1972 | UNIVERSITY OF ILLINOIS, Urbana, IL |
| | B.A. in Journalism with Advertising Emphasis |

SELECTING A RESUME FORMAT

As mentioned earlier, we strongly recommend the targeted format that you created in Part One. If you choose, however, to use a more traditional format, use the following exercise to help determine which one is appropriate for you. Check any statement that pertains to your current situation. Then compare the advantages and disadvantages for each.

CHRONOLOGICAL
(EMPHASIZES YOUR EXPERIENCE)

ADVANTAGES
___ Staying in the same field as past jobs
___ Job history shows real growth and development
___ Past titles are highly impressive
___ Name of last employer is an important consideration
___ Want to emphasize employment history

DISADVANTAGES
___ Looking for first job
___ Changing career goals
___ Have been absent from the job market for a while
___ Want to deemphasize dates
___ Changed employers too frequently

FUNCTIONAL
(EMPHASIZES YOUR SKILLS AND EXPERTISE)

ADVANTAGES
___ Looking for your first job
___ Changing career goals
___ Skills are more impressive than work history
___ Have been absent from the job market for a while
___ Changed employers too frequently

DISADVANTAGES
___ Have performed a limited number of skills in past jobs
___ Want to emphasize employment history
___ Job history shows real growth and development
___ Name of last employer is an important consideration

☞ To assemble a *chronological* resume: Go to page 61.

☞ To assemble a *functional* resume: Go to page 74.

PRODUCING A CHRONOLOGICAL RESUME

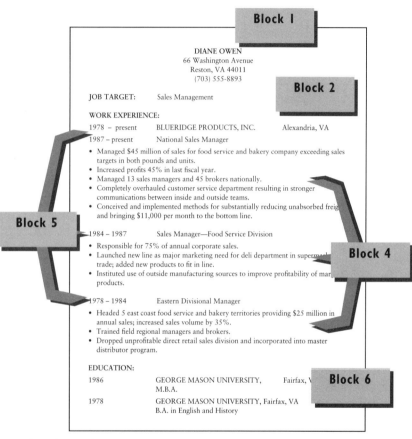

Block 1

Block 2

Block 5

Block 4

Block 6

DIANE OWEN
66 Washington Avenue
Reston, VA 44011
(703) 555-8893

JOB TARGET: Sales Management

WORK EXPERIENCE:

1978 – present   BLUERIDGE PRODUCTS, INC.   Alexandria, VA
1987 – present   National Sales Manager

- Managed $45 million of sales for food service and bakery company exceeding sales targets in both pounds and units.
- Increased profits 45% in last fiscal year.
- Managed 13 sales managers and 45 brokers nationally.
- Completely overhauled customer service department resulting in stronger communications between inside and outside teams.
- Conceived and implemented methods for substantially reducing unabsorbed freig and bringing $11,000 per month to the bottom line.

1984 – 1987   Sales Manager—Food Service Division

- Responsible for 75% of annual corporate sales.
- Launched new line as major marketing need for deli department in supermar trade; added new products to fit in line.
- Instituted use of outside manufacturing sources to improve profitability of mar products.

1978 – 1984   Eastern Divisional Manager

- Headed 5 east coast food service and bakery territories providing $25 million in annual sales; increased sales volume by 35%.
- Trained field regional managers and brokers.
- Dropped unprofitable direct retail sales division and incorporated into master distributor program.

EDUCATION:

1986   GEORGE MASON UNIVERSITY,   Fairfax, V
         M.B.A.
1978   GEORGE MASON UNIVERSITY, Fairfax, VA
         B.A. in English and History

The chronological resume emphasizes work history. A good chronological resume communicates that you are experienced and established in a particular career or profession. It demonstrates consistency.

You can use most of the information you created for your targeted resume in the chronological resume. Assemble your resume as follows:

1. CONTACT INFORMATION (block 1, page 8): Center your name and address on the top of the sheet.

2. JOB TARGET (block 2, page 10): We suggest you use a job target only if you focused the resume in that direction. If you plan to use the resume for a variety of different career directions, omit the job target. You can use a general resume without a specific objective and still make your approach more targeted by focusing on your job targets in each cover letter you write (see Power Cover Letters, page 90).

3. WORK HISTORY (block 5, page 24): Start with your most recent position and work back in time. Detail your positions of the last ten to fifteen years, stressing the most recent. You don't need to show every change within a given company. If you have had many jobs with different employers, prepare a general statement lumping several jobs under one heading.

   For each position, select three to four accomplishments that demonstrate your competence in that job. Review the accomplishments you listed in block 4 (page 22).

   If you do not have any accomplishments related to the position on your list, repeat the steps in block 4 to generate new accomplishment statements related to that job.

   Always keep your job target in mind. As you describe previous positions, emphasize those accomplishments that are most closely related to your next move up.

   Resist any temptation simply to describe duties or responsibilities. Today's employers want to know what results you produced, not what your job description was.

4. EDUCATION: List your education as presented in block 6, pages 26. If you have received a degree within the last five years, put this block right after your job target (see sample

resume on page 65); otherwise, list your education at the bottom.

5. Follow the steps for critiquing, laying out, and printing your resume given on pages 28–30.

Samples: The next few pages contain sample chronological resumes with a description about the person and the reasons he or she chose this format.

PATRICK HARGER

MARKETING/PRODUCT MANAGEMENT

As a new M.B.A. graduate from a prestigious university, Patrick's degrees were listed at the top.

Patrick's early work history indicates a move from engineering to management with a product management emphasis. It's implied in the resume that he chose an advanced degree to make himself more competitive in the professional shift.

Patrick wrote the resume with no gaps, listing his graduate assistant work as if it were a full-time job. This works to his advantage as his business school research was up to the minute and reflected a current knowledge of new developments in most businesses.

Patrick could have successfully written this resume in any of the three formats. He was most comfortable with the chronological and felt he achieved the same results while sticking with a conventional approach.

He also wrote a second, targeted resume with the emphasis on consumer protection services.

PATRICK HARGER
14 Braxton Road
St. Louis, MO 63130
(314) 555-2234

JOB TARGET: Marketing/Product Management

EDUCATION:

WASHINGTON UNIVERSITY   St. Louis, MO
1993   M.B.A. in Marketing
1982   B.S. in Industrial Engineering

WORK EXPERIENCE:

1991 – 1992   WASHINGTON UNIVERSITY   St. Louis, MO
Graduate Assistant

- Conducted a statewide survey of 750 small businesses to examine customer needs and wants.
- Coordinated in-depth interviews to identify improvement opportunities in customer support services.
- Edited incoming manuscripts and performed background research for a journal published by Washington University.
- Published over 25 articles in national journals and newsletters.

1985 – 1991   BAKER CONSULTING GROUP   St. Louis, MO
Management Consultant

- Consulted with consumer product, government, industrial, and aerospace industries.
- Presented work proposals, exhibited at trade shows, conducted telemarketing sales and surveys.
- Improved manufacturing productivity at work units in Pet Foods, Boeing, McDonnell-Douglas, and General Electric.

1982 – 1985   WELSH & WELSH, INC.   St. Louis, MO
Industrial Engineer

- Managed all industrial engineering activities for introducing new products; functioned as liaison between production, engineering, and materials control.
- Implemented world-class manufacturing techniques, including just-in-time production into assembly operations.
- Identified production and quality improvements while working as a member of quality teams.

EDUARDO HERNANDEZ

DIRECTOR OF PURCHASING—HEALTH CARE SERVICES

Eduardo had only an associate's degree, but since he moved right up the line in his career, he was ready to compete for a management position against four-year college graduates.

He demonstrated how he could achieve a good work record even as a high school graduate by putting his five years as a radio announcer in the *chronological* section of the resume. It's obvious to the reader that the gap between 1985 and 1988 was devoted to his higher education.

Since 1988 he quickly increased responsibility within two different jobs, showing sufficient reliability (at least two years on each job).

Because Minneapolis is a large metropolitan city, Eduardo had plenty of health facilities from which to choose. In this case he was targeting smaller facilities so he wouldn't be competing with an older, more experienced, better-educated work force.

EDUARDO HERNANDEZ
6790 Ellsworth Drive #407
Minneapolis, MN 55406
(612) 555-8873

JOB TARGET: Director of Purchasing—Health Care Services

WORK EXPERIENCE:

1991 – present   RYGH HEALTH CARE CENTERS   Minneapolis, MN
                   Operations Supervisor

- Supervised all functions of the Operations Department consisting of three route drivers, one repair technician, and two shipping/receiving clerks.
- Purchased all inventory and established stock levels.
- Negotiated purchase agreements with vendors to establish best pricing and to return obsolete inventory for full credit.
- Developed purchasing system to reduce inventory on hand and fill back orders more efficiently.
- Implemented procedures for transporting hazardous wastes.

1988 – 1991   ST. CLAIR HOSPITAL   Minneapolis, MN
                Supply, Procurement, and Distribution Technician

- Established and maintained stock levels of medical and surgical supplies for all hospital wards, emergency room, and surgery.
- Checked, cleaned, and sterilized instruments used for surgery and the emergency room.
- Purchased and maintained inventory stock levels for the central supply department.

1980 – 1985   KSZT RADIO STATION   Minneapolis, MN
                Radio Announcer

- Prepared and broadcast an eight-hour radio music program consisting of hourly news, weather, and sports.
- Wrote and produced commercial copy for local sponsors.
- Designed and maintained top-40 play list with Billboard of top 100.

EDUCATION:

1988   MANKATO TECHNICAL COLLEGE   Mankato, MN
                A.A. in Business Administration

CATHERINE HOLMES
Budget Analyst

Catherine's career never directly connected back to her degree. However, as a young graduate enjoying her entry-level administrative job, she seized opportunities to launch herself into a long, successful career in the world of accounting and budgets.

The chronological resume really reflects her career growth from the bottom-up, hands-on school.

Given her current job title, Manager of Accounting Operations, Catherine wore a big hat covering many functions. She now wanted to narrow her focus to budget analysis. This constituted a lateral move.

The gap between 1987 and 1988 represented a December job change that was resolved when Catherine was rehired in March. She would have been justified in closing the gap but felt more comfortable leaving it alone, explaining it in an interview if requested.

There was also a gap from 1976 to 1978, when she traveled in Europe and helped care for an ailing grandmother. However, given her fourteen years of steady growth, that gap didn't need coverup or explanation.

CATHERINE HOLMES
1456 15th Street
Harrisburg, PA 17110
(717) 555-9928

JOB TARGET: Budget Analyst

WORK EXPERIENCE:

1988 – present   A-MED MEDICAL CORPORATION   Harrisburg, PA
               Manager of Accounting Operations

- Developed complex budgets and forecasts.
- Assimilated due diligence documents for merger to create financial projections; projected effect of strategic changes on consolidated company.
- Managed and coordinated installation, operation, and training of accounting software.
- Produced financial statements, closed monthly books, reconciled general ledger.
- Standardized and managed accounts payable processing system; spearheaded audit.
- Reviewed product costs and profitability.

1980 – 1987   CYNTAC CORPORATION   Harrisburg, PA
               Regional Office Supervisor

- Performed full range of administrative and financial services including P&L review, credit and collection, personnel, general administration, and expense approval.
- Developed budget and monitoring systems.
- Managed staff of seven.
- Conceived and managed program to increase accounts receivables collections.

1978 – 1980   ADVANCED DESIGN SYSTEMS   Harrisburg, PA
               Administrative Manager

- Joined ADS at its inception as sole nontechnical team member.
- Designed accounting, operations, and administrative systems and controls.

EDUCATION:

1976   PENNSYLVANIA STATE UNIVERSITY
            B.A. in Psychology, cum laude

ANGELA J. FLANDERS

Angela completed a two-year associate's degree in a New York State community college before transferring to the University of Wisconsin. Since her full degree is most relevant and Wisconsin has clout, she named only one school.

Angela's job target was an entry-level position in marketing or management. Given that she stated her major and minor, she felt it was redundant to make a job target statement.

It is recommended to use both school and home addresses, as Angela did, when generating a resume before graduation.

To test the job market, she also wrote a functional resume where she emphasized detail categorized under the *activities* heading. Both resume formats were equally successful.

ANGELA J. FLANDERS

School Address
University of Wisconsin
111 North Harwood Court
Madison, WI 63704
(608) 555-2185 Ext. 3036

Permanent Address
14363 West Saugerties Road
Saugerties, NY 12477
(914) 555-2466

EDUCATION: UNIVERSITY OF WISCONSIN   Madison, WI
B.S. in Business Administration, May 1993
Major: Management Minor: Marketing

EXPERIENCE:

Summer 1992   VERNON SYSTEMS CORPORATION   Kingston, NY
Input/Output Control Room Clerk

- Controlled data received or distributed in information systems.
- Recorded daily and monthly accounts receivable and sales input.
- Prepared output for distributing that included bursting, decollating, and identifying recipient.
- Trained new permanent employees.

Summer 1991   ULSTER CO. SHERIFF'S MARINE DIV.   Kingston, NY
Secretary/Receptionist

- Opened and closed marine base.
- Compiled semiannual payroll report.
- Received incoming telephone and radio calls.
- Examined daily reports.
- Recorded marine violations.
- Trained new employees.

1987 – 1991   STUDIO TAN AND NAIL SALON   Kingston, NY
Receptionist/Sales

- Opened and closed salon.
- Sold tanning packages.
- Prepared tanning programs for customers.
- Set up appointments for tanning and nails.

ACTIVITIES:

- Active member of Phi Beta Lambda (business organization), 1990 to 1993
- Attended 1991 National Fall Leadership Conference, St. Louis, MO
- Residence Hall Public Relations Director, 1 year
- Residence Hall Floor Vice-President, 1 year
- Residence Hall Floor Sports Representative, 2 years

VINCENT YOUNG

CHIEF CATERER

Vincent had both the training and the experience lined up exactly for a chronological resume. He had grown steadily in three different jobs over thirteen years. His real desire was to move back to Seattle and become an executive chef on a cruise line. With only an associate's degree, he also knew this would probably be a long shot, but he prepared a targeted resume, doing all the requisite research to fill out the *capabilities* section.

He also put together a chronological resume as a backup targeted to a position as a chief caterer where there were many more employment opportunities.

The eight-month gap between 1985 and 1986 was spent studying electronics, which turned out to be totally unfulfilling. Vincent didn't want to mention it on his resume, even though he had developed some skills there.

VINCENT YOUNG
1990 Clark Avenue
Portland, OR 97207
(503) 555-4487

JOB TARGET: Chief Caterer

WORK EXPERIENCE:

1990 – present   J&R CATERING   Portland, OR
                    Chief Caterer

- Developed business sales that exceeded $228,000 annually.
- Contracted catering services for parties; held a major account to provide catering for the Portland Civic Center.
- Catered many different events from picnics to formal dinners for more than 3,500 persons.
- Managed catering services for the Vancouver Masonic Temple for one year.
- Managed staff of 50; organized jobs; ordered, prepared, and delivered food.

1986 – 1990   INNS WAY MANAGEMENT, INC.   Seattle, WA
                 Night Chef

- Supervised five chefs during night shift for two area Radisson hotels.
- Received a four-star rating by the American Automobile Association.
- Hired, trained, and supervised kitchen personnel; maintained payroll records; monitored performance.

1980 – 1985   THE GROTTO   Seattle, WA
                 Partner/Owner

- Took over a failing restaurant and in three years grossed over $2 million.
- Developed menu specializing in Cajun and Creole food.

EDUCATION:

1979   PORTLAND COMMUNITY COLLEGE
          A.S. in Applied Science in Culinary Arts

PRODUCING
A FUNCTIONAL RESUME

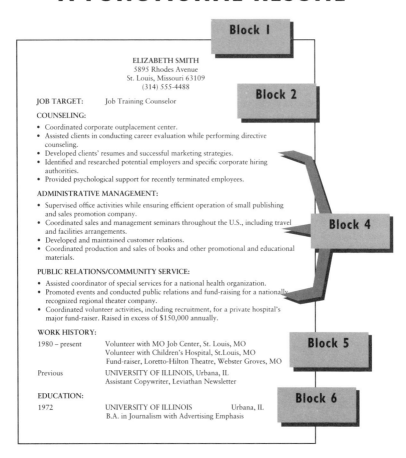

Block 1

Block 2

Block 4

Block 5

Block 6

ELIZABETH SMITH
5895 Rhodes Avenue
St. Louis, Missouri 63109
(314) 555-4488

JOB TARGET: Job Training Counselor

COUNSELING:

- Coordinated corporate outplacement center.
- Assisted clients in conducting career evaluation while performing directive counseling.
- Developed clients' resumes and successful marketing strategies.
- Identified and researched potential employers and specific corporate hiring authorities.
- Provided psychological support for recently terminated employees.

ADMINISTRATIVE MANAGEMENT:

- Supervised office activities while ensuring efficient operation of small publishing and sales promotion company.
- Coordinated sales and management seminars throughout the U.S., including travel and facilities arrangements.
- Developed and maintained customer relations.
- Coordinated production and sales of books and other promotional and educational materials.

PUBLIC RELATIONS/COMMUNITY SERVICE:

- Assisted coordinator of special services for a national health organization.
- Promoted events and conducted public relations and fund-raising for a nationally recognized regional theater company.
- Coordinated volunteer activities, including recruitment, for a private hospital's major fund-raiser. Raised in excess of $150,000 annually.

WORK HISTORY:

1980 – present	Volunteer with MO Job Center, St. Louis, MO
	Volunteer with Children's Hospital, St.Louis, MO
	Fund-raiser, Loretto-Hilton Theatre, Webster Groves, MO
Previous	UNIVERSITY OF ILLINOIS, Urbana, IL
	Assistant Copywriter, Leviathan Newsletter

EDUCATION:

1972	UNIVERSITY OF ILLINOIS Urbana, IL
	B.A. in Journalism with Advertising Emphasis

The functional resume is best used to highlight capability areas that prove you have the background necessary to do the job. You can organize your abilities in order of their relevance to current opportunities or interests, and not be governed by chronology. This gives you the flexibility to rewrite and focus your past so that you feature only what's important to a future job target.

You can use most of the information you created for your targeted resume to produce a functional resume. Assemble your resume as follows:

1. CONTACT INFORMATION (block 1, page 8): Center your name and address on the top of the sheet.

2. JOB TARGET (block 2, page 10): Include your job target if it directly relates to an employment opportunity supported by the resume. If you plan to use the resume for a variety of career directions, omit the job target. You can use a general resume without a job target or job objective and still keep yourself focused on your job targets in individualized cover letters (see Power Letters That Open Doors, page 90).

3. FUNCTIONAL SECTIONS: Include two to four sections that describe a particular area of expertise or involvement. List these functional areas in order of relevance to your current job target or career preferences.

   Start with a heading that describes this area (see the Suggested Functional Headings, page 76). Within each functional area list the most directly related accomplishments or results you produced regardless of when they occurred. Use the items you wrote in your accomplishments list (block 4, page 22).

   If you do not have sufficient accomplishments related to any selected functional area, do block 4 again and compose four to five statements that describe your accomplishments in that functional area.

4. WORK HISTORY (block 5, page 24): Start with your most recent position and work back. List only the last three to five positions of the last ten years or so. You don't need to show every position change within a single company.

5. EDUCATION: List your education as you described it in block 6, page 26. If you have completed a relevant course or received a degree within the last five years, put this block at the top (after your job target); otherwise, show your education at the bottom.

Follow the steps for critiquing, laying out, and printing your resume given on pages 28–30.

SUGGESTED FUNCTIONAL HEADINGS

Here are some functional headings. Check those that best describe your abilities and potential and are in line with your job target. Add any others that are appropriate.

___ Accounting	___ Advertising	___ Aeronautics	___ Arbitrage
___ Architecture	___ Automotive	___ Banking	___ Biology
___ Botany	___ Career Counseling	___ Chemistry	___ Child Care
___ Communications	___ Commercial Art	___ Coaching	___ Community Affairs
___ Computers	___ Construction	___ Counseling	___ Cooking
___ Ecology	___ Data Processing	___ Drafting	___ Economics
___ Editing	___ Education	___ Electronics	___ Engineering
___ Entertainment	___ Family Services	___ Fashion	___ Financial Planning
___ Fine Arts	___ Fund-raising	___ Graphic Design	___ Health Services
___ Horticulture	___ Human Resources	___ Industrial Design	___ Insurance
___ Interior Design	___ Journalism	___ Law	___ Layout
___ Management	___ Marketing	___ Mathematics	___ Medicine
___ Mental Health	___ Movies	___ Museum Work	___ Music
___ Navigation	___ News Anchor	___ Nutrition	___ Oceanography
___ Office Services	___ Photography	___ Performing Arts	___ Physical Fitness
___ Physics	___ Planning	___ Printing	___ Programming
___ Promotion	___ Public Relations	___ Public Service	___ Publishing
___ Real Estate	___ Recreation	___ Robotics	___ Sales
___ Secretarial	___ Social Services	___ Systems Design	___ Sports
___ Television	___ Textiles	___ Training	___ Transportation
___ Travel	___ Weather	___ Video Engineering	___ Writing

Add your own:

Samples: The next few pages contain sample functional resumes with a description about the person and the reasons he or she chose this format.

JOSEPH PERONE

GEOPLANNER—HAZARDOUS WASTE

Joseph had a long, successful career as a geologist. As a means of bringing his skills up to date, he studied hazardous waste management at a community college.

He had enough relevant experience in his job target area to list his past activities under *functional* categories of both geology and hazardous waste.

Given numerous job changes and a two-year stint away from his field, he was better served by a functional resume than a chronological one. He could also have developed a targeted resume for his chosen job target.

An interesting twist to Joseph's career was a short stint, including an earlier degree, in elementary education, which covered 1968 to 1972.

He left this fact off completely because it was not particularly useful to his new job target. However, Joseph should disclose such information at any significant interviews.

JOSEPH PERONE
6 Greenwald Avenue
Tumwater, WA 98502
(206) 555-3828

JOB TARGET: Geoplanner—Hazardous Waste

GEOLOGY:

- Supervised and directed drilling, logging, and coring activities during well site operations.
- Evaluated, examined, and prepared drill cuttings and core samples during well site geological investigations.
- Conducted surface mapping investigations by taking field measurements of dip and strike.
- Testified numerous times before the State Oil and Gas Commissions of Texas and Louisiana.

TECHNICAL/HAZARDOUS WASTE:

- Certified in OSHA Safety and Health Training for hazardous waste site investigations.
- Monitored CERCLA, RCRA, SARA Title III, TSCA, and other environmental requirements and regulations.
- Proficient in the theory and application of gamma, geophysical, and resistivity logs.
- Designed and created computer programs used in the development of drilling programs.
- Utilized technical writing skills and constructed graphs and charts for government use.

WORK HISTORY:

1990 – present	EXXON, USA, INC. Geotechnical Consultant	Tumwater, WA
1989 – 1990	BURGER CHEF, INC. Manager and Area Marketing Director	Tumwater, WA
1986 – 1989	MHQ CORPORATION Geological Consultant	Tumwater, WA
1976 – 1986	KUFACKER EXPLORATION CO. Area Geologist	Walla Walla, WA

EDUCATION:

Present	Tumwater Community College Major: Hazardous Materials Management	
1976	MISSOURI SCHOOL OF MINES B.S. in Geology	Rolla, MO

DORIS MOORE

TECHNICAL WRITER–EDITOR

Doris had no steady work history to show that she had had assignments using employable skills in her job target area.

Although not listed as such, most of her assignments and accomplishments came from temporary employers who had hired her for administrative positions and utilized her writing and editorial skills.

Living near a major university in Baton Rouge, she had selected courses and even teaching assignments to cover several of her diverse interests, from child care to guitar to editing.

Having raised and supported her children as a single parent, she was now ready to work full time outside the home.

Doris could have written a targeted resume, but she felt more comfortable with a functional format.

DORIS MOORE
6543 West Washington Avenue
Baton Rouge, LA
(318) 555-9202

JOB TARGET: Technical Writer-Editor

TECHNICAL WRITING:

- Provided article for *Values Forum*, an in-house magazine for The American Family Association.
- Wrote and edited nutrition column in newsletter for Bayou County Foster Parents' Association.
- Wrote, revised, compiled, and developed instruction materials for guitar students while serving as guitar instructor at Louisiana State University.
- Wrote Individual Educational Plans; composed progress reports; created lesson plans; recorded observations and parent conferences while employed as an educator.

EDITING:

- Served as editor for LSU's student literary magazine, *Chrysanthemum*.
- Created office manual, conducted correspondence, recorded meetings and other business as an administrative aide.
- Served as secretary for the Louisiana Multiple Sclerosis Association.

WORK HISTORY:

1978 – present	Editing and administrative assignments in Bayou County and LSU departments on a contract basis.
1988 – present	Self–employed as a family day-care provider Licensed as a Bayou County foster parent
1982 – present	Guitar Instructor, Louisiana State University
1982 – 1986	Group Leader, Sunburst Child-Care Center

EDUCATION:

1980 – present	LOUISIANA STATE UNIVERSITY Classes in technical writing and editing, desktop publishing, early childhood
1976	UNIVERSITY OF TEXAS–AUSTIN B.A. in English Literature

DAWN REID

MANAGEMENT AND SUPERVISION

Dawn wrote this resume with no particular job target in mind as she was retiring from her company after thirty-five years of service.

She could have written a chronological resume because she certainly had a steady job history. However, after taking a retirement workshop, she decided to categorize her work in order to present a more focused sense of her accomplishments over the years.

She also had a quiet desire to pick up a temporary consulting assignment with the company she was leaving. She wanted them to see her functions before her titles.

Her two functional categories focused only on her experience and accomplishments over the past ten years. Most employers are really not interested in your job history much farther back than that.

Some of her retiring colleagues who knew they definitely wanted consulting positions were encouraged to write targeted resumes.

DAWN REID
17 Bell Court
Morristown, NJ 07960
(201) 555-5688

MANAGEMENT AND SUPERVISION:

- Administered telephone switched-access capacity management for Massachusetts, Hartford (CT), Newburgh (NY), including current trunk usage, grade of service requirements, and correction of potential servicing problems.
- Managed AT&T International Operating Center and maintained responsibility for all international results, labor relations, all union and nonunion personnel issues, and international customer relations.
- Managed Relocation Benefits Department including home-sale plans, homes-in-inventory, and the implementation of domestic and international moving plans.
- Supervised regional implementation of Performance/Attendance Improvement Program for 17,000 participants.

PROGRAM DEVELOPMENT AND TRAINING:

- Designed information packets, audiovisual materials, seminars and face-to-face communication program for relocating employees.
- Established spouse counseling program to assist trailing spouse in finding new employment.
- Represented AT&T as speaker and panel member at relocation seminars and meetings.
- Introduced new ideas to assist relocating employees through home buyers' counseling service, videotapes of communities and homes, and customized town profile reports.
- Developed and presented seminars for 1,200 employees including internal and external coordination for salary administration, pension calculation, predecision counseling, and outplacement.

WORK HISTORY:

1958 – present	AT&T	Basking Ridge, NJ
1990 – present	Supervisor, Access Engineering	
1987 – 1990	Manager, Relocation Benefits and Pioneers	
1981 – 1987	Staff Supervisor, Relocation Benefits and Pioneers	
1958 – 1981	Various Responsibilities from Operator to Supervisor	

EDUCATION/PROFESSIONAL AFFILIATIONS:

Rutgers University	Business Courses
AT&T Training Center	Professional Development Seminars
College Intern Program	Manhattanville College, Pace University, Kings College, College of New Rochelle, Cornell University

ADRIENNE HOFFMAN

ADMINISTRATOR—INTERNATIONAL ORGANIZATION

Adrienne had a varied educational and work background. She wanted her job target to be as open as possible so she could include a wide range of opportunities, given her education and experience.

Her second function was listed as *retail administration* to prevent her from being narrowly pegged to photography or gallery administration.

Although "business manager," which is listed under FRN International, sounds like a heavy-duty executive position, Adrienne was actually an executive assistant in a four-person company, running the business while the owners took buying trips to Europe.

The *special skills* category worked very well in a functional resume. This becomes the umbrella under which she could list carefully selected skills and training that could give her an added advantage with some employers.

In Adrienne's case, a targeted resume would not have served her as well. It would have been much harder to include all of her work accomplishments without the functional subcategories.

ADRIENNE HOFFMAN
291 Central Park West #3-B
New York, NY 10024
(212) 555-3596

JOB TARGET: Administrator—International Organization

PROJECT COORDINATION:

- Managed and coordinated the packaging concept and layout of an entire computer software package, including artwork concepts, graphic design, and color choices.
- Worked with production and distribution vendors for software product.
- Arranged full logistics for company participation in quarterly trade shows.
- Researched and interviewed potential new hires.
- Provided liaison between Paris and New York, handling foreign exchange problems, travel, and other international trade issues.
- Assisted in setup, administration, accounting, bookkeeping, and advertising.

RETAIL ADMINISTRATION:

- Assisted in setting up and hanging photography gallery exhibits.
- Organized and inventoried photographs.
- Worked extensively with clients on the phone and in person.
- Handled, showed, and sold works of art.
- Organized mailing lists, books, and artists' biographies.
- Aided in artistic choice decisions for advertising and American product design.

SPECIAL SKILLS:

- Fluent in written and oral French.
- Operate movie cameras and direct short-subject stories.

WORK HISTORY:

1991 – present	FRN INTERNATIONAL Business Manager	New York, NY
1993	HOWARD HARTMANN, INC. Assistant to Gallery Owner	New York, NY
1989 – 1991	SOFT-THINK SYSTEMS, INC. Special Projects Coordinator	New York, NY

EDUCATION:

1989	VASSAR COLLEGE B.A. in Language and Literature, Photography Minor	Poughkeepsie, NY
1987	INSTITUTE DE FRANÇAIS French Language and Art History	Paris, France

GAIL HANSEN

RETAIL STORE DISPLAY DESIGNER

Gail took a bold step in choosing functional titles for her resume. Visually creative with a few impressive though diverse credits, she chose the word *envisioner* over *creator* or *designer*. Although the word was outside of mainstream resume language, she felt it was a more exact descriptive title.

The functional resume allowed Gail to pull together the diverse applications of her creative talent. Her accomplishments were spread out over twenty-three years, and the last twelve were only temporary or volunteer assignments.

In addition, Gail had no college or other relevant courses. She was a smart, capable high school graduate, but she had not supplemented her career with higher education. So she left off *education* as a category.

This choice is recommended only if one is more than ten years out of high school and there is absolutely no other education to list.

GAIL HANSEN
667 Winston Court
West Hartford, CT 06117
(203) 555-7878

JOB TARGET: Retail Store Display Designer

ENVISIONER:

- Visualized innovative methods of designing and creating imaginative environments.
- Used scrap lumber and other trash collectibles to construct different display themes; developed new ways to use existing display materials.
- Designed and constructed costumes from Goodwill finds to old hospital gowns.
- Designed stage props using various-height ladders, colored filters, and back lighting.
- Completely redecorated and remodeled two houses and an apartment, designing specific structures to fit designated areas.
- Designed and built bookshelves, storage systems, and bathroom interiors to effectively utilize available space.

SCOUT:

- Able to assemble and create artifacts from small finds.
- Dressed an entire cast with 20 yards of muslin, dyed and fashioned for each character.
- Tore up packing crates and rebuilt them to make fences and posts to use in a display.
- Decorated an entire apartment using linoleum and wallpaper bought at garage sales. Furnished apartment by getting to know trash collectors and using their knowledge in searching for good pieces.

COORDINATOR:

- Arranged new system of storing merchandise; designed inventory tracking system to prevent reordering of supplies already in stock.
- Organized a block party for 80 families; formed committee to canvass neighborhood; ordered food and drink from suppliers and arranged for food preparation; organized activities and entertainment.
- Started International Gourmet Club with rotating hostess and alternating guests.

EXPERIENCE:

1979 – present	Freelance Photographer, Community Volunteer, Homemaker
1973 – 1979	Commercial Artist for department store (Gimbel's)
1970 – 1973	Assistant Artist for publishing firm (Ludden & Ludden)

PART THREE

Opening Doors to Your Future

POWER LETTERS
THAT OPEN DOORS

To get the best possible results from your job search, every resume you send to a potential employer should be accompanied by a personalized cover letter—a power letter. The powerful cover letter is your personal introduction to a potential employer; it invites the employer to read your resume by relating it to specific real needs.

If you are sending resumes to fifteen different employers, you should prepare fifteen separate cover letters. Each letter will emphasize how your skills specifically relate to that employer's needs.

Another type of power letter is sent after each interview.

TEN TIPS FOR WRITING A POWER LETTER

1. **Write the letter to a real person.** Use the name and title (double-check spelling) of a person you want to receive your resume. If you do not know the name, call the employer to check. Be persistent. Do not address your letter to "Dear Sir" or "To Whom It May Concern."

2. **Send your letter to a decision maker**—a person who will make the hiring decision. Usually this is not someone in personnel, but a manager in the organization. You will want to find out who this person is.

3. **Refer to something special at the start.** Pique the employer's curiosity to read beyond the opening paragraph by showing you know something about the firm.

   "I was extremely impressed with the recent write-up in The Wall Street Journal *that described your company's advances in twenty-four-hour customer support systems. Your commitment to taking care of your customers has furthered my interest in learning more about your organization."*

   "Your opening for a ____ has recently attracted my attention as a way to enter the growing field of ____ . With my background in ____ , I can make a significant contribution in a short time."

   "Jim Swanson suggested that I contact you to learn more about opportunities at ____ . On the basis of his familiarity with my work, he felt that my experience in ____ would be of tremendous value to your efforts in ____ ."

4. **Focus on what you can contribute.** Find out about the employer's needs, products, competitors, contracts, and flow of business. Show how you connect with this. If you are responding to an advertisement, use words from the ad in your letter.

   "As my enclosed resume indicates, I have extensive marketing experience with Japanese investors and manufacturers. In addition, I have been studying fiber optics development at the university. My expertise can help you accelerate your plans to open up new markets in the Orient."

5. **Declare the value you have to offer.** Refer to a skill that you mentioned in your resume or brought up in the interview. Make sure the employer understands that you can provide a direct benefit.

"Knowing that the extent and quality of my contributions in the past are significant indicators of my future success with your organization, allow me to highlight some of the benefits I feel will be most relevant to your current needs..."

"In my last experience with _____ , I was responsible for the successful development of _____ . This important program was a main reason for the organization's increase in business by more than _____ . In looking at the current dynamics of your firm, I feel that by _____ in this new position, I could make a similar contribution."

6. **Express yourself!** Tell the employer you are right for the job and can contribute to the firm's success. If you don't say this, no one else will.

"The qualities you seek in your _____ candidates directly parallel those that I have consistently developed throughout my career."

"With my experience in _____ for the last _____ years, I am confident that I would be an ideal person to fit this challenging position. More specifically, I..."

7. **Close with a request for action.** Make a clear request for the action you want to see happen. Suggest an interview time or tell the employer when you will follow up with a phone call. Avoid vague endings that leave the initiative up to the employer.

"I would appreciate a few minutes of your time to discuss my qualifications. I will contact you on _____ to arrange a meeting."

POWER LETTER FOLLOW-UPS

8. **Send a follow-up letter immediately after an interview.** A strong follow-up letter is m   ore than a thank-you note. It provides an opportunity for you to reinforce and repeat the benefits the employer will receive if you are hired. It lets you present additional information not covered in the interview, and it keeps your name in front of the employer.

"Thank you for considering me for the _____ position in your organization. I enjoyed meeting you and learning more about the challenges this position offers. Based on my past experience and training, I believe I can make significant contributions to your organization. Among these are..."

9. **Don't close the door to future opportunities.** Even if you were turned down for a job, send the employer a letter to express your continued interest in working for the company. Then follow up with a phone call.

    "Although you mentioned that your company had no immediate openings in my field, I am confident I possess important qualities that could be of value to you in your attempt to _____ . As an indication of my confidence, I propose _____ ."

10. **Make it look great.** Your letter is an example of the care you put into your work. Keep your letter to one page. Check for spelling, punctuation, and grammar mistakes. Type it or print it out on good-quality bond paper (white or off-white). Send it in a matching envelope.

1433 Washington Avenue
Boston, MA 02345
9 June 1993

Ms. Susan Jones, Assistant Manager
Computer World
134 Beacon Street
Boston, MA 02478

Dear Ms. Jones:

I saw your notice in the Boston Globe about the customer service position for Computer World. The qualities you need closely match ones I've developed. I have four years of experience with computer systems, and I'm sure my skills would be of use to you right away.

I know that a successful service representative has to take care of customers in a way that is helpful and efficient. These are characteristics that I've developed in organizing and presiding over our school's computer users' group. Members in this group must thoroughly know DOS and Macintosh computers and provide service to other students in the school. Last year we served more than five hundred individuals and consistently received high ratings on the quality of our services from our clients.

I am confident my knowledge and abilities will be of value to your company. I request a few minutes of your time to discuss my qualifications. I will contact you next Friday to arrange a meeting. If you have any questions in the meantime, please call.

Best regards,

Leroy Alexander
(617) 555-5678

March 19, 1993

Dr. Robert Sayers, President
Seattle Community College
12 Rocky Mountain Road
Seattle, WA 98101

Dear Dr. Sayers:

My firsthand experience on the administrative staffs of two colleges should be of interest to you in your new drive to centralize functions at SCC.

The enclosed resume will give you the highlights of my experience in handling the specific administrative problems of college departments. Of special interest is my turning over ten years of filing into an easy-access database in a record-breaking six months (including a complete staff training).

We are moving to Seattle at the end of this school year. I will be in your city from April 10 to April 24. If possible, I would like to arrange an appointment during that period to discuss your new organization and explain how my experience may be beneficial. I will call you shortly.

Yours very truly,

Diane Tims
344 West Erie Street
Scotia, New York 12992
(518) 555-3882

TWENTY HOT TIPS FOR MANAGING YOUR CAREER

1. **Design your own future.**
   You are responsible for the way your life works out. Your future will be determined by how well *you* deal with the multiple variables of economy, politics, globalization, and personal capability. Do not let others tell you how impossible it is to get the work you want. Statistics measure how others are doing. You can have what you want if you create your own vision of your future, in spite of the doubts of others.

2. **Love your work, love your life.**
   The satisfaction provided by your work life directly affects the quality of your entire life. Seek out work that brings you personal satisfaction and relates to your personal interests and beliefs. Growth, development, and sometimes even personal wealth will follow your commitment to have a high-quality working life.

3. **Express your uniqueness.**
   You represent a unique combination of skills, interests, experiences, and abilities. You are not adequately defined by a job title or a degree. Find ways to describe and define your uniqueness in a way that sets you apart. Show how your special qualities offer employers a special benefit.

4. **Study the market.**
   The job market is a dynamic, changing sea of opportunity. Read journals and books about several related fields. Join a professional association. Use the library and keep a journal.

5. **Turn problems into opportunities.**
   Employers don't give out jobs because people need them. Jobs exist because there are problems to be solved. New jobs are created all the time as consumer demands, competition, and technology change. You vastly improve your ability to attract

employers' interest when you present yourself as a problem solver.

6. Follow the *Universal Hiring Rule.*

> *Any employer will hire any individual if the employer is convinced that the hire will produce more value than it costs.*

There is always an opportunity for a person who knows how to create value.

7. **Learn to earn.**
   It is essential to continue to develop your skills and ability to be able to deliver value to an employer and enhance your career. Stay current with changing technologies even if they're not required in your current job. Keep looking beyond the boundaries of your current job or profession.

8. **Build networks.**
   The best way to find out about job opportunities and to get inside for interviews is knowing someone in the field. With good networking, you can expand the circle of people you know, or can reach, who can tell you what is happening in a field, make introductions, and give you advice.

9. **Be a high performer.**
   High performance equals job mobility and salary growth. Make sure everything you do is done well and has an impact on the success of your department or organization. Know the strategies of your organization and look for ways to tie what you are doing to what is important. Don't wait for the annual performance evaluation. Seek out areas for continuous improvement.

10. **Invent your next job.**
    A job is an opportunity to solve a problem. Since there is no shortage of problems, there is no shortage of job opportunities. Stay in touch with what people in your field are concerned about. Ask to take on new assignments as opportunities develop, not just for promotion but also to keep redesigning your job to keep it relevant.

11. Explore the hidden job market.

Eighty percent of the available jobs on any given day are not advertised. By focusing primarily on the want ads you limit your search to jobs everyone already knows about. Get the names of all the potential employers in the field and contact them for developing any future openings.

12. Make more money.

Money follows value: This is the fundamental rule about money. To earn more money you must produce more value (turn a department around, eliminate two steps in the production process, persuade customers to come your way). Negotiate salary on the basis of what you are worth, not what you need.

13. Reject job security.

Rapid changes in the marketplace, competition, and technology cause continual restructuring of organizations, often with layoffs. It is a mistake to depend on one job or even one field or industry for career and personal financial security. Consider your job as a "project" and build an inventory of new experiences, capabilities, and contacts from it. Always keep your resume updated and your network active. Interview with other employers regularly—at least every two years.

14. Be relentless.

To get what you want takes continual work and activity: contacts, requests for interviews, new assignments, attempts to meet certain people. Often you will experience turndown and rejection. Don't take this personally. The best job searches looks like this: no, no, no, no, no, no, no, no, no, no, no, no, YES.

15. Ask tough questions.

Challenge old assumptions and beliefs. Ask people in the field for their interpretation of what is happening. Get candid feedback on how you are doing. The quality of your questions indicates the quality of your thinking.

16. Be an entrepreneur.

More corporate activities are moving out of the company environment to small independent suppliers, contractors, or consultants. The largest job growth comes from growing new businesses. Consider how you can package your capabilities into your own business. By working for two or three different employers as a consultant, you enhance growth opportunities and spread your risk.

17. Follow a plan.

Don't just let your career blindly lead you. After you have decided what you want in your career vision, then lay out the steps to make it happen. Put your plan to paper and share it with someone else who will help keep you on track. If you are not keeping pace with your plan and time line, modify your plan.

18. Never stop the job search.

A career is your lifetime relationship with work. Even if you are satisfied with the job you have, keep looking ahead and to the sidelines at what else is available within the company or in other firms. The biggest loyalty you owe is to your own personal and professional development. This does not mean you should be disloyal to your employer; it means not to depend on his or her loyalty to you.

19. Perfect your presentation.

Be able to speak well of yourself and to look like a success. Project what you believe in a way that gets others to listen. Practice your presentation and get feedback on how you come across.

20. Be outrageous!

Break your own (smaller) image of yourself. Step out of old assumptions, opinions, and beliefs about yourself. Be willing to see yourself as a success even when circumstances are running the other way. Assert your worth even beyond what you have proved. Avoid small personal put-downs or disclaimers—they can be self-fulfilling.

KEEPING TRACK OF YOUR CONTACTS

A stack of resumes sitting on your desk will get you nowhere fast. Get your resume and a power cover letter into the hands of the decision makers. These are people within organizations who have the power to hire you.

You can get the names and addresses of prospective employers in your job target area from a variety of sources at hand. These include:

• Business directories at your local library
• The Yellow Pages
• Your local chamber of commerce
• Want ads in back issues of newspapers
• People in your network who can suggest potential employers
• Company listings in the college placement council's annual
• Information from professional and trade associations

Assemble a list of employer prospects in your job target area and select the ones you want to target for interviews. Call each organization to get the name of the manager of the department in which you would likely work. Bypass the personnel office.

Compose a power cover letter that clearly states your interest in the employer and the value you can contribute to lead your resume to your prospect.

Follow up your letter after five days by calling the person by phone. Keep calling until you reach him or her.

When you make contact, stress the value you communicated in your letter and ask for a meeting. If you get an objection, acknowledge it and repeat your request for a meeting.

If you make no headway, thank the employer for his or her time. Send a follow-up letter in a few weeks enclosing some information that may be useful or interesting to the employer, such as an article from a trade publication. Keep requesting a meeting. Be persistent but not obnoxious.

If you still haven't changed the situation after the third attempt, put this contact on the back burner. Direct your energy elsewhere.

Do not lose track of your prospects. Keep a 3"x 5" index card on each employer that contains the key information you need to know. Use the following as a template for your cards:

Business/Organization: _____

Contact Name: _____

Position: _____ Department: _____

Address: _____

Phone: (___) _____ Fax: (___) _____

Secretary's name: _____

Date Contacted: Reason:

_____   _____

_____   _____

_____   _____

(Notes and comments on back)

In addition, keep a Contact Log of all employers who have received your resume. Use this to keep track of who's active or inactive of the employers on your prospect list.

CONTACT LOG

Date Sent	Contact Name	Business/Organization	Phone	Active	Inactive	Comments